Dennis Woodward 22/5/84

NO, MINISTER

NO, MINISTER

by Hugo Young and Anne Sloman

British Broadcasting Corporation

Published by the British Broadcasting Corporation,
35 Marylebone High Street, London W1M 4AA

ISBN 0 563 20056 1 Hardback
ISBN 0 563 20105 3 Paperback
First published 1982

Set in 10/12pt Linotron Palatino by Input Typesetting Limited
and printed in Scotland by Thomson Litho Limited, East Kilbride

Contents

Acknowledgements

We owe a debt of gratitude to Sir Ian (now Lord) Bancroft for his encouragement of this enterprise; to Sir Patrick Nairne especially, for taking it seriously and encouraging his colleagues to take part; to the numerous civil servants who assisted, both on and off the air. At Broadcasting House we thank Karen Henderson, Rosemary Phillipson and, in particular, Janet Smith who typed the manuscript – and guarded it even while being mugged one night.

Preface

These programmes originated in a subversive idea. Serving civil servants had very rarely appeared on radio or television, and had never contributed publicly – outside occasional darting forays to Select Committees in the House of Commons – to a discussion of the function and efficiency of the civil service. By early 1981, however, Whitehall had had more than eighteen months' experience of a government which appeared to be more hostile to the civil service than any in recent history. This hostility had several aspects. To begin with, the Conservative party under Mrs Thatcher had become dedicated while in opposition to reducing the size of the public sector generally. Within this broad definition the civil service, of course, occupied a central place. Indeed, one of the few beliefs which united all wings of the Tory party was that Whitehall was wasteful, over-manned, self-protective and deeply uninterested in managerial efficiency. But alongside this scepticism about the sheer size of the service there was something else: a suspicion of senior civil servants (otherwise known as mandarins) as the repositories and defenders of the kind of conventional, centrist wisdom that Thatcherism was dedicated to challenging.

This, besides being an interesting moment to look at British administration, presented an opportunity. Perhaps, in the most discreet and mannerly way, top civil servants would welcome an occasion to reveal themselves to a wider public as men not quite so contemptible as Conservative politicians, by their generalised attacks, were tending to make them sound. Out of this possibility, *No, Minister* grew. Nobody, of course, was so vulgar as even to hint at such a motive. Through our work at the *Sunday Times* and the BBC, we both knew a number of senior civil servants. In previous years we had collaborated in several series of radio programmes about the law, in the course of which we had penetrated another bastion of the British establishment and persuaded High Court judges, for the first time, to contribute to broadcast discussions about topical legal controversies. In trying to persuade the mandarins to do the same, we had invaluable help from within the machine. But the person we had to convince was the head of the service, Sir Ian Bancroft.

In conversation Sir Ian was surprisingly positive, but it soon became apparent that there were limits to his enthusiasm. The programmes were acceptable in principle, but there must, of course, be conditions. The following exchange of letters is worth reproducing not because it ended in 'victory' for the BBC, but because of the light it throws on the anguished concept of free broadcasting entertained by Whitehall – and on the distance Sir Ian was ultimately prepared to travel in order to meet the BBC's conditions. On 27 February 1981 Sir Ian wrote:

> Dear Mrs Sloman,
>
> I am pleased to be able to tell you that ministers have agreed to serving civil servants taking part in your projected series of programmes on the Civil Service. Some conditions are attached to this agreement however – none, I think, onerous – and I will need your assurance concerning them before we can proceed any further.
>
> Since the CSD has been charged with co-ordinating the participation of civil servants, we shall need to know well in advance whom you propose to interview in each programme and to see a final version of the plan for each programme as soon as possible. A list of the relevant questions should be provided to each serving civil servant (and to us centrally) at least 48 hours in advance of recording; and, at least a week before transmission we shall need to know the context in which each interview by a serving civil servant will be broadcast. I assume that the interviews with serving civil servants will not be split up and used in different programmes unless the interviewee has been approached in advance and has agreed.

Bancroft added that he would provide a liaison officer who would suggest 'suitable interviewees' and sit in on all the interviews. He concluded: 'We are naturally anxious to do all we can to make this an interesting and worthwhile series.'

By BBC standards, the proposed conditions were certainly onerous: intolerably so. On behalf of the Corporation Anne Sloman replied in terms which, while acknowledging that final approval would have to come from the Prime Minister, asserted that Sir Ian's demands would make for thoroughly bad radio:

> Dear Sir Ian,
>
> Thank you for your letter. I am delighted to know that we now have the official go-ahead for my proposed series on the civil service.
>
> I was more than a little surprised by the conditions laid down in your second paragraph. Naturally, I understand your necessary apprehensions about the programmes; we

shall, after all, be breaking new ground. We discussed this very frankly and fully at our meeting of 3 February and the conclusions we reached that day on the best way to proceed, should the PM give us the go-ahead, bear little relation to those laid down in your letter, nor to the realities of effective programme-making. Please may I take your points one by one:

1. '. . . we shall need to know well in advance whom you propose to interview in each programme . . .' There is no problem with this. I have discussed my ideas already with Sir Patrick Nairne and Sir Brian Hayes and we have thought about possible interviewees within their departments. As I mentioned to you on 3 February, I am also planning to involve Sir Brian Cubbon and Sir Donald Maitland.

2. 'A list of the relevant questions should be provided to each serving civil servant (and to us centrally) at least 48 hours in advance of recording.' As I explained to you when we spoke, Hugo Young would telephone everyone taking part in the programme about a week before the interview to go over the area of questioning. This has the advantage not only of giving the participants plenty of time to think about their answers but also an opportunity to voice any worries or queries they may have about the proposed content, and to suggest points we may not have thought of. We are not attempting to throw our interviewees with trick questions, but fresh ideas and supplementaries usually occur as you go along. If a civil servant does not wish to answer a question he can always refuse to do so, and his refusal would of course not be used in the programme. There is another practical objection to written questions. Their corollary is usually written answers, or at any rate, carefully prepared unspontaneous answers, and these will jar terribly in any programme, giving exactly the stuffy, pedantic impression of civil servants that you and I agreed this series would be setting out to dispel. A good interview must sound like a conversation, and it won't, unless it is. I would add, incidentally, that in the fifteen years in which I have worked in broadcast journalism, I have only been asked for written questions on two previous occasions; in both instances the request came from totalitarian regimes abroad who had good reason to fear the spontaneous interviewing which has long been the tradition in Western democracies.

3. '. . . we shall need . . . to see a final version of the plan for each programme as soon as possible.' Again this was a point I thought we had gone over in some detail at our meeting. I pointed out to you that the outline I had prepared was a starting point for the series, but that

> good programmes were made in the making and the final shape should emerge as the material is collected. The editing of a good radio programme goes through several stages and final adjustments are often not made until the studio session just before transmission. I have a deep distrust of the school of journalism that starts off with fixed ideas and a predetermined conclusion and then tailors the facts gathered to fit in with it. Hugo Young and I expect to learn a great deal about the civil service in the course of this series and I hope that the final product will reflect this. Let me give you a concrete example. On our original plan I envisaged bringing some examples of our dealings with Brussels into several of the programmes. After talking to Sir Patrick Nairne and Sir Brian Hayes (who were both extremely helpful) I decided this wouldn't work; we would do better to devote a separate programme to this subject.
>
> 4. '. . . at least a week before transmission we shall need to know the context in which each interview by a serving civil servant will be broadcast.' Naturally I appreciate why people should be nervous about the way their material will be used in a documentary format. As I understood it when we talked, you agreed that in practice there is no alternative but to trust the good faith of the producer. I have never received a complaint about taking an interviewee's words out of context or otherwise violating the sense of what he wanted to say. It would of course be made absolutely clear to those taking part which programme they were being interviewed for – there would be no point in doing otherwise.

There followed a silence. A few days later, a civil service strike, long debated and long put off, finally began, and Sir Ian's Civil Service Department was wholly occupied with it. A one-day strike of selected workers on 9 March grew into a guerilla campaign of strikers across the entire civil service. This strike, which was to last twenty-one weeks (longer than any other strike in Britain since the miners' strike in 1926) became a regular background accompaniment to our interviews. It wasn't in fact over until after the last programme was broadcast. Everywhere we went – but particularly at the CSD itself and at the DHSS office in Newcastle – it was impossible to escape its disturbance and the anxiety it caused. None was more anxious than Bancroft, but on 20 March he replied gracefully. By the extent to which he came round to the BBC's point of view one can perhaps gauge the seriousness of his desire to have something broadcast – however it turned out – which would give civil servants a chance to reveal themselves at their best, in an arena where they were not accustomed to being heard:

> Dear Mrs Sloman,
>
> I am sorry I have not replied sooner to your letter of 4 March, but as you might imagine, the last two weeks have been fairly hectic in the Civil Service and particularly within the CSD.
>
> In the meantime you have seen the Lord President and the Minister of State. I hope that from these meetings and from all your other recent encounters in Whitehall you are in no doubt of our good will and good intentions. I did not intend, by the conditions I set out in my letter to you of 27 February, to hinder you in your programme making but to ensure that you would be providing us with an essential minimum amount of information about the programmes themselves as they were being prepared. But I do of course accept your professional judgement on the effect those conditions, as they stand, would have on the enterprise.
>
> In the light of your observations, therefore, I am content for serving civil servants to be interviewed provided that you let our Chief Press Officer, Bert Jarmany, know as far as possible in advance which serving Ministers and civil servants you are arranging to interview; and that, as you have undertaken in your letter, Hugo Young will let the prospective interviewee know at least a week in advance, what ground he proposes to cover in the interview.
>
> I am grateful for your reassurance that if a serving civil servant would find a particular question embarrassing, he may decline to answer and that his refusal will not be used in the programme.[1]
>
> While I accept that you will be shaping these programmes right up to the point of transmission, it would nevertheless be helpful if you could let me have a more up-to-date notion of the general contents and shape of the series when you have got them more in focus. Perhaps you and Mr Young could have a chat with me about this at the appropriate time.
>
> Finally, so far as the context in which the interviews with serving civil servants are to be used is concerned, I would not dream of questioning your good faith. But I felt it necessary to draw your attention to what I think is a genuine difficulty and to the potential hazards that exist

1 In the event this reassurance was, as we suspected all along, unnecessary. We interviewed twenty civil servants for the series; not one refused to answer a question put to them, although some answers naturally fell short of total frankness.

> for the individual civil servants who are interviewed for programmes which also include interviews with Ministers and other politicians. All I would ask is that you take account of this point when you come to the stage of finally assembling and editing your interviews into programmes.

It remained to select and approach suitable contributors. Having secured Bancroft's co-operation, we decided to exclude all civil servants who had retired and confine ourselves entirely to those still in post. On the political side we followed a similar principle, interviewing only serving Conservative ministers, and recent Labour ministers who had every reason to expect to be ministers again. This, while enhancing authenticity and authority, had a side-effect we had not anticipated. By limiting the contributions of those who fell into neither of these categories (to, for example, former political advisers and those like William Plowden, now head of the Royal Institute of Public Administration, who had also seen the system from the inside), we also limited the truly critical voices. Those who had previously gone on the record as vociferously anti-civil service were those on the outside – back-benchers and academics, for example – and we concluded that an unreservedly critical view could only be sustained by those who had never been seduced by the undoubtedly luxurious personal service which Whitehall provides for politicians who serve in government. This was a point, incidentally, picked up by the junior minister for the civil service, Barney Hayhoe, while being questioned one day in the House of Commons. He was being challenged on Conservative attacks against the civil service during the strike, and replied: 'I repudiate the Honourable Gentleman's comments about attacks on the civil service. Why does he not listen to the radio programme *No, Minister* on Sunday evenings? He will then discover the considerable contribution that our civil service makes to the running of the country.'[1]

One other, somewhat eerie, note should be recorded. Along with the civil service strike, another running story during the making of these programmes was the much-debated future of the Civil Service Department itself. The Conservatives were known to dislike the department, and a substantial study was set in train, under the aegis of Sir Derek Rayner, to examine

1 *Hansard*, HC, Vol. 7, No. 130, col. 580, 29 June 1981.

the implications of abolishing it and transferring its functions to the Treasury. When this was first recommended, it was turned down by the Cabinet, mainly, it was said, because senior Treasury ministers were reluctant to take on a new and substantial responsibility. It seemed that the CSD had been spared. In November 1981, however, this proved to have been a short-run victory. The Prime Minister announced that the department would indeed be abolished, but instead of its functions all going to the Treasury they would be divided between the Treasury and the Cabinet Office. The most conspicuous victim of this decision – otherwise greeted with virtually unanimous approval in the press – was the Permanent Secretary, Sir Ian Bancroft. This was a very rough way for Sir Ian to go. He had another year to pass before he was sixty. There was no more dedicated upholder of the ethos of public service, or more committed defender of the civil service itself. The move was seen by the vast majority of civil servants as another example of the government's vendetta against them. To Sir Ian, the winding up of the CSD was a personal affront – as, in part, it was probably intended to be.

The Participants

Abel-Smith, Professor Brian.
b. 1926. *Educ.* Haileybury; Cambridge. Professor of Social Administration, University of London at the London School of Economics 1965–. Special adviser to the Secretary of State for Social Services 1968–70, 1974–8; to the Secretary of State for the Environment 1978–9.

Bancroft, Sir Ian.
b. 1922. *Educ.* Coatham School; Oxford. Entered Treasury 1947. Permanent Secretary at the Department of the Environment 1975–8. Head of the Home Civil Service and Permanent Secretary at the Civil Service Department 1978–81.

Barnett, Rt Hon. Joel.
b. 1923. *Educ.* Manchester Central High School. Labour MP 1964– . Chief Secretary to the Treasury 1974–9. Member of the Public Accounts Committee 1965–71, Chairman 1979– .

Benn, Rt Hon. Tony.
b. 1925. *Educ.* Westminster; Oxford. Labour MP 1950–60, 63– . Postmaster General 1964–6. Minister of Technology 1966–70. Secretary of State for Industry 1974–5. Secretary of State for Energy 1975–9.

Brown, Sandra.
b. 1949. *Educ.* Bede Girls Grammar School; London University. Entered Department of Energy 1974. Principal 1977– (in Coal Division 1980–).

Butler, Sir Michael.
b. 1927. *Educ.* Winchester; Oxford. Entered Foreign Service 1950. Deputy Under-Secretary of State at the Foreign Office 1976–9. Ambassador and UK Permanent Representative to the European Communities 1979– .

Crowe, Brian.
b. 1938. *Educ.* Sherborne; Oxford. Entered Foreign Office

1961. Counsellor and Head of Chancery in the Office of the UK Permanent Representative to the European Communities 1979– .

Cubbon, Sir Brian.
b. 1928. *Educ.* Bury Grammar School; Cambridge. Entered Home Office 1951. Permanent Secretary at the Northern Ireland Office 1976–9; at the Home Office 1979– .

Donoughue, Bernard.
b. 1934. *Educ.* Northampton Grammar School; Oxford. Senior Policy Adviser to the Prime Minister 1974–9. Development Director *Economist* Intelligence Unit 1979–81. Assistant Editor, *The Times* 1981–2.

du Cann, Rt Hon. Edward.
b. 1924. *Educ.* Woodbridge School; Oxford. Conservative MP 1956– . Economic Secretary to the Treasury 1962–3. Minister of State, Board of Trade 1963–4. Chairman Public Accounts Committee 1974–9, Select Committee on Treasury and Civil Service Affairs 1979– .

Fogden, Michael.
b. 1936. *Educ.* UK and overseas Grammar Schools. Entered Ministry of Pensions and National Insurance as temporary Clerical Officer 1955. Assistant Private Secretary to Secretaries of State at the Department of Health and Social Security 1970–8. Assistant Secretary and Head of Central Pensions Branch, Child Benefit Branch and Overseas Branch, Newcastle-upon-Tyne Central Office 1979– . National Chairman of First Division Association 1981– .

Hanson, Neil.
b. 1923. *Educ.* City of Leeds School. Entered civil service as junior clerk, Leeds Public Assistance Committee 1939. Under-Secretary at the Department of Health and Social Security, Controller Central Office, Newcastle-upon-Tyne 1981– .

Hattersley, Rt Hon. Roy.
b. 1932. *Educ.* Sheffield City Grammar School; Hull University. Labour MP 1964– . Minister of State, Foreign and Commonwealth Office 1974–6. Secretary of State for Prices

and Consumer Protection 1976–9. Opposition spokesman on the Environment 1979–81, on Home Affairs 1981– .

Hayes, Sir Brian.
b. 1929. *Educ.* Norwich School; Cambridge. Entered Ministry of Agriculture, Fisheries and Food 1956. Permanent Secretary at the Ministry of Agriculture, Fisheries and Food 1979– .

Hayhoe, Barney.
b. 1925. *Educ.* State schools; Borough Polytechnic. Conservative MP 1970– . Minister of State, Civil Service Department 1979–81. Minister of State for the Civil Service at the Treasury 1981– .

Healey, Rt Hon. Denis.
b. 1917. *Educ.* Bradford Grammar School; Oxford. Labour MP 1952– . Secretary of State for Defence 1964–70. Chancellor of the Exchequer 1974–9. Opposition spokesman on the Treasury 1979–81, on Foreign Affairs 1981– .

Heseltine, Rt Hon. Michael.
b. 1933. *Educ.* Shrewsbury School; Oxford. Conservative MP 1966– . Minister for Aerospace and Shipping 1972–4. Secretary of State for the Environment 1979– .

Hordern, Peter.
b. 1929. *Educ.* Geelong Grammar School, Australia; Oxford. Conservative MP 1964– .

Maitland, Sir Donald.
b. 1922. *Educ.* George Watson's College; Edinburgh University. Entered Foreign Service 1947. Chief Press Secretary, 10 Downing Street 1970–3. Ambassador and UK Permanent Representative to the EEC 1975–9. Deputy to the Permanent Under-Secretary of State at the Foreign Office 1979–80. Permanent Secretary, Department of Energy 1980– .

Milne, John.
b. 1922. *Educ.* Bede Grammar School. Entered War Office as clerical officer 1939. Senior Principal and Head of Department of Health and Social Security, Child Benefit Branch in Washington, Co. Durham 1978– .

Nairne, Sir Patrick.
b. 1921. *Educ.* Radley College; Oxford. Entered Admiralty 1947. Deputy Under-Secretary of State, Ministry of Defence 1970–3. Second Permanent Secretary, the Cabinet Office 1973–5. Permanent Secretary at the Department of Health and Social Security 1975–81. Master of St Catherine's College, Oxford 1981– .

Nodder, Timothy.
b. 1930. *Educ.* St Paul's School; Cambridge. Entered Ministry of Health 1954. Deputy Secretary at the Department of Health and Social Security 1978– .

Partridge, Michael.
b. 1935. *Educ.* Merchant Taylors'; Oxford. Entered Ministry of Pensions and National Insurance 1960. Under-Secretary at the Department of Health and Social Security 1976–81. Deputy Secretary and Principal Establishments Officer 1981– .

Paxman, Giles.
b. 1951. *Educ.* Malvern College; Oxford. Entered Department of the Environment 1974. First Secretary at UKREP, Brussels 1980– .

Plowden, William.
b. 1935. *Educ.* Eton; Cambridge. Entered Board of Trade 1960. Lecturer at London School of Economics 1965–71. Central Policy Review Staff, Cabinet Office 1971–7. Under-Secretary at the Department of Industry 1977–8. Director-General Royal Institute of Public Administration 1978– .

Pooley, Peter.
b. 1936. *Educ.* Brentwood School; Cambridge. Entered Ministry of Agriculture, Fisheries and Food 1959. Minister (Agriculture) in the Office of the UK Permanent Representative to the European Communities 1979– .

Price, Christopher.
b. 1932. *Educ.* Leeds Grammar School; Oxford. Labour MP 1966–70, 1974– . Chairman, House of Commons Select Committee on Education, Science and the Arts 1980– .

Prior, Rt Hon. James.
b. 1927. *Educ.* Charterhouse; Cambridge. Conservative MP 1959– . Minister of Agriculture, Fisheries and Food 1970–2. Leader of the House of Commons 1972–4. Secretary of State for Employment 1979–81. Secretary of State for Northern Ireland 1981– .

Rayner, Sir Derek.
b. 1926. *Educ.* City College, Norwich; Cambridge. Joined Marks & Spencer 1953. Joint Managing Director 1973– . Special Adviser to HM Government 1970. Chief Executive, Procurement Executive at the Ministry of Defence 1971–2. Adviser to the Prime Minister on improving efficiency and eliminating waste in government 1979– .

Soames, Lord, Rt Hon. Christopher (Life Peer 1978).
b. 1920. *Educ.* Eton; Sandhurst. Conservative MP 1950–66. Secretary of State for War 1958–60. Minister of Agriculture, Fisheries and Food 1960–4. Ambassador to France 1968–72. Commissioner of the European Communities 1973–7. Lord President of the Council 1979–81.

Walker, Rt Hon. Peter.
b. 1932. *Educ.* Latymer Upper School. Conservative MP 1961– . Secretary of State for the Environment 1970–2. Secretary of State for Trade and Industry 1972–4. Minister of Agriculture, Fisheries and Food 1979– .

Williams, Rt Hon. Shirley.
b. 1930. *Educ.* St Paul's Girls' School; Oxford. Labour MP 1964–79. Minister of State, Education and Science 1967–9, Home Office 1969–70. Secretary of State for Prices and Consumer Protection 1974–6. Secretary of State for Education and Science 1976–9. Social Democrat MP 1981– .

The Civil Service is too Powerful

First Broadcast: 14 June 1981

The title of the famous television series *Yes Minister*[1] was a piece of calculated irony. The 'Yes', of course, was meant to be read as 'No'. Behind the deferential image conveyed by civil servants saying 'Yes Minister' lurked the truth, which was that this fawning servility was pure pretence. While saying 'Yes', Sir Humphrey and his boys were doing the opposite. The civil servants, in other words, were running the country their way, only going through the motions of doing what their minister thought he'd been elected to do. *No, Minister*, this radio series, sets out to explore with real politicians and – which is much more rare – real civil servants this real-life hypothesis.

It comes at a time when the civil service is more unpopular than it's ever been: more lowly regarded for its inefficiency, its excessive size, its faceless lack of accountability, its part of the blame for landing the country in the mess we're in. We'll be looking at all these charges in turn, but will start by asking, 'Is the civil service too powerful?' Its power is certainly fabled, especially its negative power – its extremely sophisticated capacity, as Tony Benn depicts it, to pretend that it's on a minister's side when really it's batting for itself.

Benn:

The deal that the civil service offers a minister is this: if you do what we want you to do, we will help you publicly to pretend that you're implementing the manifesto on which you were elected. And I've seen many ministers, of both parties actually, fall for that one. They go along with what is presented to them. Now of course, civil servants will tell you, and I think it's true, that they are a clockwork motor that has to be wound up all the time, and that if there is

1 *Yes Minister* was a highly successful comedy series by Jonathan Lynn and Antony Jay which was first broadcast on BBC 2 on 25 February 1980. It depicted the adversarial relationship between Jim Hacker, the Minister for Administrative Affairs (played by Paul Eddington) and his Permanent Secretary, Sir Humphrey Appleby (played by Nigel Hawthorne), in which Sir Humphrey usually, though not invariably, emerged victorious.

> not some decisive winding-up process, the civil service runs down. But having said that, they are always trying to steer incoming governments back to the policy of the outgoing government, minus the mistakes that the civil service thought the outgoing government made.

From a typical senior civil servant – Sir Donald Maitland, Permanent Secretary at the Department of Energy – that picture may elicit fleeting recognition, but hastily followed by chilly and adamant rejection.

> *Maitland*:
> I think that's a rather clever proposition and I suppose there may be a grain of truth in it, but I'm not sure that any serious civil servant would actually approach his work in that frame of mind. I think that civil servants know perfectly well what happens when, under our system, one party succeeds another in government. No, that's a rather neat phrase, but I'm not sure that it would be foremost in the minds of civil servants.

Sir Donald is a member of the Whitehall *corps d'élite*: a body of men infrequently heard from in public. We're on a journey through the corridors of power that's never been taken before, in the company of mandarins and ministers publicly discussing the real, as distinct from the textbook, version of the British constitution. The textbooks put the matter simply, rather as Sir Donald implied. Civil servants, they say, are there to serve, and ultimately to obey, the politicians. When governments change, the civil servants neatly switch course overnight, ready to do their new masters' will. Sir Brian Hayes, who runs the Ministry of Agriculture, sums it up in four bland sentences.

> *Hayes*:
> Civil servants ought not to have power because we're not elected. Power stems from the people and flows through Parliament to the minister responsible to Parliament. The civil servant has no power of his own. He is there to help a minister and to be the minister's agent.

Listening to that, you'd have no reason to know that Brian Hayes, a Permanent Secretary before he was fifty, is reputed to be one of the most brilliant men in Whitehall. Within this subtle, clever mind, however, there seems to be genuinely very little cynicism. When offered Tony Benn's picture of the civil service as a rival in power to the politicians and a hotbed of strongly entrenched opinion, Sir Brian appeared not to recognise it.

Hayes:

This is sometimes believed and alleged. I myself don't believe it for a moment. It certainly ought not to be so and I don't think it is so, though I can speak with authority only of my own department. I think the job of the civil servant is to make sure that his minister is informed; that he has all the facts; that he's made aware of all the options and that he is shown all the considerations bearing on those options. It is then for the minister to take the decision. That is how the system ought to operate and that is how I think, in the vast majority of cases, it does operate.

Brian Hayes's present political boss is Peter Walker, the Minister of Agriculture. He, too, sees the work as a team job between official and politician, although he concedes that there can be exceptions.

Walker:

You can obviously have exceptions – a Permanent Secretary, or a leading official, or a department that has a very strongly entrenched position. For example, this department has a tradition, going back decades, of scientific and animal welfare advisory services to the farmer. If a minister came into this department whose idea was to eradicate all that, who said it was no function of a department like ours to give advice to farmers, I think that the department would present very strong arguments as to why they thought that was a very foolish policy to pursue. So there are departmental traditions which might occasionally confront a politician's viewpoint, but they are purely a result of the accumulated wisdom and experience of those departments, as opposed to the new ideas of the politician.

The starting-point of this delicate relationship is the party manifesto. It seems to be common ground that civil servants do read these documents, unlike most other members of the community. To Mr Benn, however – and remember, he's a very experienced minister, as well as a polemicist – the civil servants have positioned themselves, from the beginning, for battle.

Benn:

During an election campaign they really de-couple themselves from their ministers, disconnect except for day-to-day business. They read the manifestoes, they then prepare papers designed to show how part of them could be implemented and how part of them can't be implemented.

> They dress it up so that an incoming government will feel that there is a sympathetic civil service. In effect what they do, however, is to write massive briefs, which are the most important documents to be found in Whitehall, in which – and it's the only time it happens – they actually set out the civil service policy. And reading those, which you normally do in a great hurry when you become a minister, means that you don't really notice until you look at them later – and I have always gone back and looked at them again – what the civil service is really all about and what they want you to do. So it's partly true that they read the manifestoes and prepare documents on them, but it's also partly true that this is the one time when you get from Whitehall a single document stating what its policy is.

As you might expect, this seminal moment in our constitutional life is described somewhat differently by the Head of the Home Civil Service, the topmost mandarin of all, Sir Ian Bancroft.[1]

Bancroft:

> I believe that the real picture is this. You have major parties fighting an election; you have manifestoes written in indelible ink; and those manifestoes are studied with great consuming care by the civil service during an election campaign. Various briefs are written and placed in appropriately coloured folders – being as sure as one can, that they go into the right coloured folders – and when the government of the day then takes office, the briefs are exchanged, views are exchanged and arguments take place. Sometimes these arguments are about whether or not a particular policy should be pursued. The policy may be one which has been manufactured while the new government was in opposition without the benefit – if benefit it is – of the advice of the old pros who've been in and around this business for quite some time. On those occasions one does have arguments with a new administration.

To these arguments the civil service brings, if nothing else, a great deal of experience. As Sir Ian says, they're old pros.

1 Five months after this programme was first broadcast, on 12 November 1981, the Civil Service Department was abolished and its functions divided between the Treasury and the new Management and Personnel Office. Sir Ian Bancroft was prematurely retired, and the post of Head of the Home Civil Service was to be held jointly by the Permanent Secretary to the Treasury and the Secretary to the Cabinet. Sir Ian became a Life Peer in the 1982 New Year's Honours List.

Governments come and go, but the service goes on for ever. What Mr Benn sees as the almost conspiratorial furthering of a political position, civil servants would define as 'confronting an incoming government with reality'. Along with 'options', 'reality' is a favourite word among civil servants. And to be fair to them, most of the politicians we spoke to agreed that this, in the end, was the main road-block to a lot of their grand ideas. However, it's also the experience of other politicians, as Peter Walker said, that departments do have views. And, according to Shirley Williams, it's nonsense to imagine that civil servants themselves don't have opinions.

Williams:

It's certainly true that they have many many views of their own, and the extent to which those views are consensus views or not, in my experience, depends almost entirely on the department. The Home Office used to, and I don't suppose it has changed much, have a view very much coloured by the fact that it mostly deals with the forces of authority – prison officers, police and all the rest of it. So you've got in the Home Office profoundly conservative views of society. I found the DHSS which, by the nature of things, was most admired when it pushed on with some major social reform – like the National Health Service, like the superannuation plans, like the personal social services – to be a department that rather prided itself on being full of bright new ideas, radical proposals and so forth. It's in a sense too simple to suggest that consensus is what the civil service likes within departments. It may like that as a general ethos of the service, and probably does. But within departments you get, I think, quite a considerable marked preference for a government to the left of centre or to the right of centre, and that depends on the department.

Many civil servants recoil at even this limited concept of a departmental identity. The Home Office has been called worse things than conservative – negative and reactionary, for example. But to Sir Brian Cubbon; the Permanent Secretary, it's little more than a collection of individuals, discharging an almost bloodless professional task.

Cubbon:

Departments are efficient or inefficient – that's a fair test to apply to them – but I think if you try to judge them in policy terms you fall into a trap. I don't think that a

> department can be described as negative and reactionary. I don't think that it is a meaningful description of a department. It's meaningful of ministers, if that is the view, and it's still a subjective view that you take of the policies and the results that they produce, but not of a department.

Well, wait a minute. Was Sir Brian seriously saying the Home Office has no continuing view about, say, immigration? Surely it possessed a store of wisdom which amounted to a view?

> *Cubbon*:
>
> There's a store of wisdom about what the facts are; about what the implications are of changes in procedure; what the consequences are of certain statements, or of certain policies that might be used; and I dare say that you would find a collective and uniform statement in the department of what that assessment was. Whether that leads inescapably on to a policy, I very much doubt. For instance, I certainly don't know the views taken by, say, the six most senior people in the immigration department about what our immigration policy as a whole should be.

In the Department of Health and Social Security, by contrast, it appears that there are departmental views which the department makes real attempts to press upon an incoming minister. The Permanent Secretary there is Sir Patrick Nairne.[1] Here one certainly does get a whiff of departments – most benignly no doubt – persuading ministers that what the department wants to do happens to accord with what the minister would have wanted to do all along, had he but known all the facts.

> *Nairne*:
>
> When there's a change of government the new ministers coming into power will find that many of the things they want to do have been going on already, particularly perhaps in a social policy department like the DHSS. You'll find that there will be objectives relating, for example, to policies affecting the elderly, policies affecting the mentally handicapped, where a new government may want to give it a new slant but where a good deal is going on already. Now, in that situation I think there is often a tendency on the part of the civil servant to say, 'Look, we've got these particular plans in hand. They were just, you know, coming to fruition. They do accord very closely with what you're

1 Sir Patrick Nairne retired as Permanent Secretary in July 1981.

> after, don't they?', and in effect to try to maximise continuity. Sometimes ministers accept that. When they have a chance to know what the facts are, they sometimes think that the existing plans are exactly the plans they want.

At the opposite extreme, one should not forget, are the departments of total agnosticism. Seductive though it is, and verifiably true in some cases, to believe that Whitehall's opinions transcend the capacity of any political party to alter them, the large failures of the past also have to be accounted for, especially economic failures. It would not be the Treasury, according to Denis Healey, which united to stop a Labour Chancellor of the Exchequer from carrying out a socialist economic policy.

> *Healey*:
> I would say that of all the departments the one which has the least coherent view of its role is the Treasury. It may have been true in the ten years after the war that all Treasury officials knew exactly how the country should be run, but in my experience none of them knows now. They're deeply divided on many of the central issues. You'll find monetarist officials, people who are neo-Keynesians, people who are pragmatists of one sort or another. I would say that the only constant thing in the Treasury is a desire to see that the figures add up, and that is not always a first priority for the ministers.

It's also a great mistake to view the power of Whitehall as if the place were monolithic.

> *Healey*:
> Departments disagree with one another very much, don't forget, and some departments notoriously fight through the ages with one another – Defence fights both with the Treasury and with the Foreign Office, to take a very obvious example in the field I know well. No, I don't think that that is true. I think that a minister who complains that his civil servants are too powerful is either a weak minister or an incompetent one.

Here we reach the great riposte to the charge that the civil service is too powerful. Again it echoes the textbooks, and again it comes from both sides of the divide. In the end, it says, power lies with ministers – and devolves to officials only when ministers fail to use it. If a minister knows his own mind, the whole system, on this reading, moves smoothly into action beneath him. One way of categorising ministers, in fact, might be between those who see the system arrayed to defeat them – Dick Crossman's view, from his diaries,[1] and also Tony Benn's – and those who see it waiting for them simply to press the right button on the great Rolls-Royce machine that is Whitehall. Michael Heseltine, Secretary of State for the Environment, belongs, perhaps predictably, to the latter school, and sees the relationship between civil servants and their minister clearly.

Heseltine:

> Their job is to give him advice, the best that they can. That advice is by nature going to be cautious, and I would guess that in the vast majority of cases, it is the right advice. Of course, the responsibility of a minister is to listen carefully and evaluate that advice, and make his own judgements as to whether it fits the circumstances, and to realise that if he's going to achieve the results that his political priorities demand, he is going to have to lead that machine. The machine is not there to be a Tory machine, any more than it's there to be a Labour machine. It is there to be a very effective, dedicated and conscientious administrative machine, which the politicians have got to lead. A politician who wants to achieve what he wants must understand that.

When it was put to Roy Hattersley – now, one remembers, almost a veteran of Labour governments – that nevertheless civil servants might fight even a determined minister, elegant tooth by elegant nail, he attached roughly the same importance to ministerial machismo as Michael Heseltine did.

Hattersley:

> I'm not sure the fight is always as elegant as you suggest; I think sometimes it's a very bruising knock-out, knock-down, drag-out fight. But certainly they sometimes fight for what they believe is the right policy, and sometimes they're blinded by their own convictions into thinking that they're not interfering with policy, that they're not involved in politics, they're just talking that sort of common sense which they have been brought up to believe transcends party differences. But then that's up to a minister to overcome. I think it's a weak minister and a weak-minded minister who is more than irked by that sort of opposition. To use that as an excuse for not doing what a minister

1 Richard Crossman, *The Diaries of a Cabinet Minister*, Hamish Hamilton and Jonathan Cape, 1975.

wants to do, to use that as a reason why party policy hasn't been put into operation, is really a minister looking for reasons to excuse his failure.

This has become something of a Whitehall truism. But it rather begs a question. Before the end of the day arrives, and the buck stops with the minister, the facts have to be established. But what exactly are the facts of any situation? This is itself a highly controversial question, giving great power to those who have to answer it, and offering the potential for real trouble, particularly, as Patrick Nairne concedes, if civil servants are at odds with their minister.

Nairne:

It's often said that power does lie in having the information. I do feel that I would be a bad Permanent Secretary if I didn't have the information or was not in a position to secure information from the department on any matter which concerned the minister. My information may very often be ahead of his information and may often be wider than his, at least at the outset, because I've got the resources at my disposal. I do think that power can often lie, in theory, in the way in which civil servants, so to speak, can manipulate information. But I don't feel that I have a power that can in any way override the power of my own minister, provided that the minister makes quite clear what he wants, and provided that he trusts the senior civil servants who are working with him. I think that where things can sometimes go wrong is if there is a break in confidence between ministers and those who are working with them, so that officials are using the resources they've got with a discretion that perhaps the minister wouldn't wish them to have, in pursuing matters in a way that doesn't fit in with the minister's policies.

Even a strong minister is vulnerable to this kind of manipulation. Jim Prior is a very strong minister and, as it happens, is carrying out policies which are in harmony with those believed in, after long years of experience, by his department, the Department of Employment.[1] He has the highest regard for his civil

---

1 Three months after this programme was first broadcast, on 14 September 1981, there was a Cabinet reshuffle and James Prior was moved to the Northern Ireland department. He was replaced by Norman Tebbit, who took a tougher line on trade union legislation, more in accordance with the Prime Minister's own thinking.

servants, but he's well aware of what they could do to manoeuvre against a policy they did not like.

Prior:

They could slow it down by raising constant objections, saying that every single policy issue, however small, had to be cleared in a minute sort of way, and having endless discussions on it. That's the first thing they would do. The second thing that could be done is that they could stir up other departments to raise all sorts of objections when it went to Cabinet Committee or Cabinet. The third thing they could do, and undoubtedly this would happen, would be to have some discreet briefing of various organisations in the country to raise problems of 'Was this right?' and so on and so forth. And then lastly, of course, it somehow does get into the newspapers. I'm not saying that there would be deliberate leaks, but there would certainly be nods and winks given that the policy the minister was pursuing was perhaps rather dangerous and not according to the advice he was receiving. I think there would be a number of ways in which that could be done, and if the civil service does get at odds with a minister, then it is not very easy for either to operate very effectively.

Patrick Nairne says he has no knowledge of such a nefarious way of carrying on.

Nairne:

I've often heard this said, but I must honestly say that I've never come across it in that form at all. Civil servants are always anxious in case ministers do take decisions, particularly perhaps in Cabinet where civil servants are not in a position to open their mouths, on the basis of inadequate facts. They're nervous about a situation in which ministers may say afterwards, 'But you didn't tell us.' I think civil servants, across the board of Whitehall, do keep in close touch to make sure that the facts are right, but I must honestly tell you I've never known a situation where civil servants were working together in that kind of way – how shall I put it? – to conspire to defeat ministers' political objectives.

Nor has Sir Patrick's opposite number at the Home Office, Sir Brian Cubbon. On the other hand, is he perhaps putting into well-laundered Whitehall words something of the same thing that Jim Prior was talking about?

Cubbon:

The dialogue between officials and ministers is a more complicated subtle set of occasions than perhaps the textbooks imply. It's not a question of a single piece of paper that says, 'The proposition is *x*. The objections to it are *a*, *b* and *c*. It's clear that *x* is pretty crazy', dropping it on the minister's table and seeing what he makes of it. In a good department there will be a more careful approach to the issue, because on so many issues things like presentation, tactics, outside consultation, substance, policy and the draftability of legislation are not separate issues, they all merge together.

What Sir Brian said then, added to what Patrick Nairne hinted at a moment ago about what happens when ministers and officials fall out, gets near to a subtle description of what happened to Tony Benn, with whose experience the programme began. We discover a gloss on the simple injunction to ministers to be strong. They must also be united and, above all, at one with the Prime Minister. Michael Heseltine puts it very brutally.

Heseltine:

The Benn picture is, of course, one of the classic rationalisations of personal failure. The reason why Benn achieved nothing is because Wilson was determined he was going to achieve nothing. He put him in a ministry, surrounded him with people who didn't agree with him, and made absolutely sure that the hare-brained policies which he alone – or not he alone, but he very substantially in a minority – believed in were not pursued. It was the triumph of political will of the majority of the Labour government that hemmed Benn in, and, of course, Benn now tries to blame the civil servants. It's got nothing to do with civil servants. It was Wilson and the Labour movement who disagreed with Benn that stopped him pursuing his ideas.

But actually it turns out that Tony Benn himself agrees with this as a description of what happened when he took over at the Department of Industry in 1974. He is inclined to shift the blame from Permanent Secretaries as a breed to the whole political structure of which they are but a part.

Benn:

You're quite right in saying that a Permanent Secretary who thinks that a Prime Minister doesn't approve of a minister's policy will then undermine that minister, and

> Antony Part,[1] my Permanent Secretary at the time, did quite fairly say that Mr Benn's problem was that he was a radical minister in a non-radical government. However, that also answers your first question, which is that civil servants don't believe the manifestoes, because if they believed the manifestoes, they would feel some sense of commitment to the policy upon which the government was elected. In 1974 I was faithful to the manifesto, but the Prime Minister did not support the manifesto upon which he had been elected. Therefore you had the power of the Permanent Secretary uniting with the power of the Prime Minister who was actually unconvinced by, and felt himself to be uncommitted to, the manifesto upon which he, as well as myself, had been elected. So that's the complexity of it. It's very important not to look to the Permanent Secretaries as scapegoats, though of course they will use their influence to try to divert a Prime Minister from what he wants to do, as well as a minister, but it's much harder if they're dealing with a Prime Minister and he is committed to the policy.

The Permanent Secretaries will no doubt be delighted to hear that they're not the scapegoats after all. So there is some common ground between them and a radical politician. Did Sir Ian Bancroft, mandarin of mandarins, see himself as a man of power?

Bancroft:

> I think I would say to that, 'Up to a point, Lord Copper',[2] though I don't regard myself as one of the most powerful chaps in the country or anything of that sort, because we work subject to the views of ministers of the day.

What the civil service is about, they say, isn't power but argument, reality, meticulous attention to detail. While not necessarily at all sinister, let alone unconstitutional, this can be pretty salutary. To an idealistic minister, bounding into the Home Office, eyes ablaze with a passion for change, Permanent Secretary Brian Cubbon must come as something of a dampener.

---

1 Sir Anthony Part was Permanent Secretary at the Department of Industry 1974–6.

2 This phrase cropped up several times in our conversations in Whitehall. It is a quotation from Mr Salter, foreign editor of *The Beast* in Evelyn Waugh's *Scoop*: 'Mr Salter's side of the conversation was limited to expressions of assent. When Lord Copper was right he said, "Definitely, Lord Copper"; when he was wrong, "Up to a point." '

Cubbon:

Over the years we're all to some extent anaesthetised by the practicalities of our work and we therefore tend to see the practical aspects of idealistic policies rather clearly, and it's right, I think, that that view, that corrective, should be applied. I don't mean a corrective policy, I mean a corrective to the mental approach that goes into the making of policy, and I certainly wouldn't wish the use of the word 'corrective' to be interpreted in any sense as the beginning of obstruction. I would stand by the words I've used about the mental approach.

Corrective or not, what Sir Brian is describing is unmistakably a struggle. It may not be between Permanent Secretaries and their ministers, whose relationship is often close and trusting. But it is between the forces for change – which is what most politicians think they are concerned with – and the forces which say they've seen it all before: the people who know all the angles, worry about the sums not adding up, hate taking risks. A good many politicians resent this process, but equally there are some civil servants, like Sir Ian Bancroft, who would contend that far from being too obstructive, the service had not been obstructive enough: which strikes one as a particularly revealing, honest and plausible statement.

Bancroft:

I think there's a case to be made that over the last umpteen years we've not really argued hard enough, which explains perhaps some of the discontinuities in policy. This is where one's got to strike the balance. I can remember some years ago, in my salad days, arguing with a minister so hard that he threw the telephone at me, but having played cricket I was able to catch it and hand it back to him politely.

How appropriate to end this programme with the image of minister and mandarin throwing the telephone at each other. And the mandarin recalling his proud days on the cricket field to demonstrate his mastery. The telephone is the tool of the Whitehall network as well as, in this case, a metaphor for responsibility. Responsibility is a subtle and interesting notion which keeps cropping up in any consideration of what the civil service is really about. It is very much at issue in the most common and politically popular charge against the civil service – that it is too big and far too inefficient. That is what we shall consider next.

The Civil Service is too Big

First Broadcast: 21 June 1981

The size of the public service has grown, is growing and ought to be diminished. If any one slogan most aptly encompasses what Mrs Thatcher's government stands for, then that surely is it. Also within this obsession is a narrower, even more compelling one: the need to cut down on the number of bureaucrats. Until the civil service was overtaken by the first major series of industrial disruptions in its history, in 1981, this imperative need to cut their own operations dominated the lives of top civil servants. It also largely defined their relationship with their ministers. 'Cutting the fat out of Whitehall' is one nostrum favoured by the entire spectrum of Conservative backbenchers. One of them, Peter Hordern, the Member for Horsham and Crawley, is atypical only in that he is calm, civilised and well-briefed.

> *Hordern*:
> I divide this into two parts: first of all, the total number of civil servants, the ones who work in our ministries up and down the country, and then there are the other civil servants, who are workers in the National Health Service and under our education authorities. And it is the latter, let us say the workers in the field, who have expanded so enormously during the last twenty years. Let me give you one example of the scale of movement: between 1960 and 1978 a million people moved out of the private sector and one and a half million people moved into public-sector employment. Now that is a vast change by any standards; it makes a demographic revolution in some senses.

In trying to grapple through the words of several Permanent Secretaries and Cabinet ministers, with this question of whether the civil service is too big, we're asking not only that question but also another one. Are civil servants, who are ultimately responsible for managing these other millions of public servants in the health service, the education service and so on, capable of doing so efficiently?

One could be forgiven for supposing that this was a new question, with such an air of excited discovery do some politicians now talk about it. Indeed, I came across one stunning piece of evidence to suggest that it might be. This was the figure for the cost of having a government at all: the cost before a single school or road is built, a single welfare benefit paid out, a single shot fired out of the Ministry of Defence's ammunition stockpile. This, it recently came to light through the inquiries of Sir Derek Rayner, the Marks & Spencer efficiency expert (of whom more later), is no less that £8.3 billion.[1] That turns out to be the annual sum paid out for staff, travel, office overheads and pensions, as the price of keeping the government in place before it actually delivers anything. But if this is a new number, the numbers game itself is as old as Whitehall and so, according to Bernard Donoughue, head of the political unit in 10 Downing Street during the Wilson and Callaghan governments, is the cynicism which lies behind that phrase, 'numbers game'. In the end, he says, the civil service never cuts itself.

Donoughue:

If you analyse the process by which public expenditure cuts happen or don't happen, and where the burden falls, you can see a recurring pattern, a quite fascinating pattern, which would be amusing if it was not sad. It's a pattern that I call off-loading, or 'anybody else but us'. It's a process whereby the administrators deciding on the allocation of the cuts push the cuts to the periphery, as far away from themselves as possible. Stage one will be to push the cuts into the private sector. They are called public expenditure cuts, but they're actually cuts on capital, and they end up as private industry cuts because they're cuts on building and construction and heavy engineering and so forth, and in the end the public sector remains protected and all that happens is lots of building workers become unemployed.

But that, of course, may not be enough.

Donoughue:

Then the next stage is to off-load to the semi-government agencies. So the Foreign Office will put its cuts on the BBC Overseas Service; it will put its cuts on the British Council;

---

1 This figure, which Sir Derek revealed in conversation with us, was later confirmed in House of Commons Memoranda accompanying evidence to the Treasury Sub-Committee, 15 July 1981. House of Commons Paper No. 360, Part 5, p. 87. In his Budget statement to the House of Commons on 9 March 1982 (*Hansard*, HC, Vol. 19, No. 73, col. 740) Sir Geoffrey Howe disclosed this figure had risen in the previous 12 months: 'Out of total spending of £105 billion in the current year, the government's running costs amount to over £12 billion.'

> if pushed hard, it will put its cuts on foreign-born consuls, on anybody but those in the Foreign Office. The Department of Energy would put its cuts on the specialists, on the off-shore petroleum services, people who are actually generating revenues and generating business.[1] The Department of Environment would put its cuts on provincial museums, and so it goes on. You off-load to the periphery. If forced to make more cuts, the generalist will put the cuts on to the specialists who are not quite them, so then cuts are made in statisticians, in the economic advisers, in the scientists, anybody but the central people who are in fact negotiating the cuts.[1]

In other words, self-protection at all costs. Also from those Labour years, Denis Healey offers a more peremptory verdict – of sheer incompetence.

> *Healey*:
> I think the great weakness of the top civil servants is that very few of them are trained in management, and they don't really know how to run an operation which involves a very large number of people.

Even Healey admits, however, that this is changing. Irrespective of governments, the Ministry of Defence, which he ran for six years from 1964 to 1970, presents what is inescapably a management problem – it has well over half a million personnel. The mandarins simply had to produce a manager or two, and duly did so.

> *Healey*:
> I think things have changed. If I could give a personal example, my private secretary at Defence was a young naval chap called Patrick Nairne, who'd been responsible for naval equipment, brilliant glutton for work but passionately interested in management. Now he's been the Permanent Secretary of the biggest single management department outside Defence, which is DHSS, and I think he's doing it quite well. The trouble is that you really need

1 This was later denied by the Permanent Secretary at the Department of Energy, Sir Donald Maitland, who told us that: 'In the Department of Energy between April 1979 and April 1981 staff was reduced by 6% overall. The reduction in the administrative group was 9.4%, the biggest cuts being at Principal and Senior Principal level. Over the same period the number of Petroleum Specialists increased by 6.8%, the Professional and Technology Group increased by 37% (an overall increase of 19% in the Professional and Technology Group, including the Petroleum Specialists); and there was no change in the number of scientists.'

trained managers at every level, and we do not have training in management in Britain the way they have it, for example, in the great schools, les Grandes Ecoles, in France.

This self-same Patrick Nairne is now very much at the centre of the government's efforts to reverse the course of history as Bernard Donoughue and a lot of other people, in both parties, have wearily seen it. The civil service itself, Mrs Thatcher has decreed, is to be cut from 700,000 to 630,000 employees by April 1984, ten per cent in five years.[1] The DHSS, where Sir Patrick is Permanent Secretary,[2] has 100,000 employees. Fifteen thousand have got to go, and not simply by eliminating their functions. The department will be obliged to become more efficient and its Permanent Secretary, as he says, will have to deploy what, in the life of a Whitehall high-flier, is a relatively new talent.

Nairne:

I was looking the other day at a book on the civil service, published in 1951,[3] and found that there was no mention of management in the list of contents, and that management didn't even feature in the index. In general, I think it's since the Fulton Committee Report in 1968[4] that management has become a very much bigger part of life for those at the top of Whitehall. I myself have got a very big department to manage, but I do also have a fairly strong team to help me manage it.

Even so, he personally gives a great deal more time to management than did his predecessors twenty years ago.

Nairne:

When I talk about the job of a Permanent Secretary, I attribute about thirty per cent of my time to the management task compared with about forty or fifty per cent of my time to policy work.

---

1 In his Budget statement to the House of Commons on 9 March 1982, the Chancellor of the Exchequer Sir Geoffrey Howe said: 'The whole cost of Government administration does indeed impose a formidable burden upon the taxpayer . . . This is why we set ourselves the task of reducing the size of the civil service from 732,000 in 1979 to 630,000 by April 1984. We are on target. Numbers are down already by 57,000. We now have the smallest civil service for 15 years.'
Hansard, HC, Vol. 19, No. 73, col. 740, 9 March 1982.

2 Sir Patrick Nairne retired as Permanent Secretary in July 1981.

3 T. A. Critchley, *The Civil Service Today*, Victor Gollancz, 1951.

4 *The Civil Service*, Vol. 1. *Report of the Committee*, 1966–8. Chairman: Lord Fulton (Cmnd. 3638). HMSO, 1968.

After talking to quite a few of these characters now, I have little doubt that those who run the civil service do strive for efficiency, are conscious of cost, would like to do better – especially now the government has told them to. They do not, in fact, accord with the popular image, offered by academics and politicians, as well as much more vulgar types, of spendthrift, bloated irresponsibles. The Department of Energy has only a fraction of the staff of the DHSS[1] but its Permanent Secretary, Sir Donald Maitland, thinks he's as vigilant as any profit-conscious managing director in the private sector. He has some very practical ways of keeping a watch on costs.

Maitland:

For example, I am very concerned about the amount of paper which is generated. I am keen, and I'm sure most of my colleagues share this view, that as many matters as possible should be dealt with either on the telephone or by a meeting walking along the corridor, rather than initiating a piece of paper. I am also concerned, and I think we all are in this department, about the numbers of copies which are made of documents. The circulation lists tend to grow, and they tend to be sanctified by being repeated. One has to ask constantly, 'Do these people on that list really need to know?' If not, strike their names off.

Back at the DHSS, Patrick Nairne's chief managerial lieutenant is Michael Partridge, at forty-five already a Deputy Secretary, the second rung from the top. Ninety-six thousand of the department's hundred thousand are under his command, the vast majority of them in that absolutely archetypal civil service activity, administering social security. Here is the really sharp end of the numbers game, and here the man who has to persuade himself that he is keeping his vast army up to the mark.

Partridge:

You must have a system which measures the amount of work you do, which monitors it, which measures it against the resources of manpower that you're putting into it, and gives you indicators of some sort by which you can measure the efficiency. You haven't got a profit motive like you have in private industry, and therefore it's a more difficult task in the public service. What you have to do is to set up

---

1 In April 1981 the Department of Energy had 1198 staff (excluding ministers and casual staff) and the Department of Health and Social Security had 97,412.

targets for people to achieve, and then measure whether they achieve them or not. If they don't, you then have to take measures to improve the efficiency. If they do, you try to see whether there are still further improvements you can make. These targets have to be set in consultation with the staff officers. There's no point in setting an impossible target which people can't reach. Equally, there's no point in setting a very easy target. We've been working on this over the last ten years and we now have quite a sophisticated way of measuring the work of each local office and the manpower it uses, week by week. This is studied by managers in local offices and then in the regions and then at headquarters every week and every month, so that we can tell very quickly whether efficiency is going up or down and take measures accordingly.

To pursue this thought, we decided to visit the greatest barony in Mr Partridge's domain. If we're talking about numbers, Whitehall itself is not the place to be. More than eighty per cent of the civil service works outside London altogether; a good few of them on what has become a kind of campus of the welfare state, in and around Newcastle-upon-Tyne. Here you move from the so-called corridors of power to mile upon mile of the corridors of joined-up nissen huts, where they look after everyone's pensions; and the shiny modern corridors, over in Washington New Town, where Child Benefits are logged, scrutinised, authorised and despatched. Through the eyes of Neil Hanson, a man whose leathery experience has taken him from the old National Assistance Board, through running hostels for refugees from Suez and Hungary, now to be controller of the Newcastle empire, one soon puts into perspective any vague feeling that there just *must* be too many bureaucrats. Bureaucracy does have rather a lot to do.

Hanson:

For instance, we hold forty-eight million records of contributions paid during people's working lives. We post to Contribution Records some thirty-eight million individual contribution returns from employers every year. We answer sixty thousand inquiries about the contents of those records every day. We pay benefits to seventeen million people who draw those benefits every week, every month or every quarter. To do that, we are renewing order books, for instance, at the rate of nearly a million a week. We pay

> people who live overseas too, about a quarter of a million of them, and we also deal with all questions that can arise as a result of people going overseas during their working lives.

What impressed us about Newcastle was something we honestly had not expected. We've been into quite a number of offices and factories between us. Walking around this enormous welfare estate, with its vast array of computers, its row upon row of computer operators, its paper stored by the ton, its clattering printers and its almost forbiddingly earnest supervisors, one could not recall ever before witnessing quite such dedicated industry applied to such boring work. The manager on the ground there is Mike Fogden, an Assistant Secretary in the DHSS, and a living emblem of Whitehall's at least spasmodic desire to send people away from London to learn about operations in the field.

> *Fogden*:
> It's certainly true that some of my contemporaries assumed that I'd been sent to the Siberia of DHSS when I was asked to come to Newcastle Central Office. On the other hand, there's a growing feeling, one to which I subscribe, that senior civil servants should experience operational situations, either within the civil service itself or even within industry, by going out on secondment.

But it's still unusual for the top civil servants to move away from the home counties.

> *Fogden*:
> The outlets in the operational field, although they do exist, tend generally to be filled by people who live in the areas in which they work. In effect one could perhaps say that Newcastle Central Office, in that respect, is a self-perpetuating oligarchy. When I came here I was told it was rather like the Labour Party – you didn't join it, you were born into it. When you go around the site you come across three generations here; there are grandfathers, fathers and sons working on the site.

If one were being hyper-critical – perhaps pretending to be a Tory MP – one might have wondered why, on the Newcastle site, quite so many civil servants were available to escort us on our tour. But in fact they were just desperately keen to show off their operation. One could also make a quite unfair joke about the number of tea trolleys we saw – it was just that we happened to be following the tea-break from corridor to corridor. On the whole everything Neil Hanson says is believable.

Hanson:

We've just got to be efficient, because if we get things wrong we affect such a large number of people. For instance, if we are wrong in only one per cent of our contributions posting every year, we affect about 400,000 people straight away, so they get into difficulties later when they want to claim benefits. If we're wrong in only one per cent of our payments, 150,000 people suffer, or more. So it's very important indeed that by and large we get things right – and it's not by and large, we do get things right to a very very high degree. To make sure that we do, we have constant monitoring of the quality of our work and we're always looking at our systems to see whether we can improve them. Of course, one of the big things that we think about during the course of our monitoring is whether we can do things more cheaply; we don't want to spend any more money on administration than we absolutely have to.

And what is the incentive for that?

Hanson:

The incentive is that we want to run an efficient operation, and running an efficient operation means that we do it at the lowest possible cost. We are all taxpayers, so if we are efficient we cost the taxpayer, including ourselves, less.

But is that quite convincing? One's not doubting for a moment that this is what the civil servant who is in charge of large bodies of men wants to achieve. All that Mr Hanson is saying, however, is that, within the framework he is given, he is doing his best.

It's become clear during this inquiry that if one is asking *seriously* whether the civil service is too big, the framework is what should be questioned. Mere waste is only a small part of the point. The real issue is: is civil servants' work, and are their rules, really necessary? It may be different in the health service and the education service, but as far as central government goes most disciplines are certainly observed. But Sir Derek Rayner suggests they may not be what matters. He is the man brought in by Mrs Thatcher from the private sector to scrutinise and improve efficiency all across Whitehall.

Rayner:

Those disciplines are, to my mind, too much in the nature

of, 'Has the work been done correctly according to the rules and regulations which are laid down?' It is not the kind of examination that I am accustomed to which is, 'Are all the rules and regulations necessary?' And it's this which stands in the way of reform because you cannot, as a civil servant carrying out a task, bring about those changes in the rules and regulations. Not only do they apply to the department in which the civil servant may be working, but more often than not, because there's more than one department involved, there's also legislation to consider, and many outside interests who would be affected if changes were made without consultation. So, no, they don't examine things in the way that I think they ought to be examined.

Nor, Sir Derek thinks, is it enough simply to be aware of the numbers problem.

Rayner:

Taken as a whole, they are conscious about their numbers. They do really believe, in many cases, and indeed could give chapter and verse, that the numbers they employ are those needed to deliver the task. My main complaint, apart from the rules by which they work, is that there are too many lines of hierarchy that get involved in the delivery of the work. There's too much monitoring of the work and this, to me, unnecessarily absorbs people's time.

Too much monitoring, too many layers of hierarchy? Whatever the truth about that, we now do have a government openly committed to cutting down. And whatever the zeal of the civil service, as it would claim, in seeking efficiency all the time, Sir Ian Bancroft, the head of the service, is candid enough to admit that it is Conservative politicians who have provided the real stimulus. For why, one must surely ask, has all this not happened before?

Bancroft:

A good question, one that I have been asked on several occasions, often by parliamentarians. I think the answer is that there has been, in fact, a minimal movement downwards in the civil service, which started certainly in 1976 when the Labour government published a white paper[1] on public expenditure, saying that they were proposing to cut the costs of the civil service by £140 million. I think the

1 Treasury *Public Expenditure 1979–80*, (Cmnd. 6393), HMSO, 1976.

reason why it's got an added dimension with this government is that they've put it right at the top of their programme, and now size and efficiency are the two watchwords of the day. And rightly so too, I think.

But exactly where the politician fits into this is a rather puzzling question. Clearly the Tory party has provided the political incentive, but to what extent are ministers ready to see themselves as managerial scourges? They are responsible for their departments, yet in a way they are not fully in charge of them. Certainly, to an old stager like Lord Soames, the Minister for the Civil Service[1] and a man who was in government as long ago as 1955, before Mrs Thatcher even got into Parliament, modern ministers live in a world that's not quite what it was.

Soames:

Much more management goes on today, but I suppose this is true in the country as a whole. There's much more emphasis on tight-ship management all over the country than there was, I think, in those days. A lot of expressions which never existed then have now become part of the jargon, like 'management control'. Certainly management plays a far greater part today in the thinking of ministers and occupies ministers much more than it did in my first incarnation as a minister in the fifties and sixties. We spend much more time talking about the civil service in Cabinet today and about making it more efficient, and I think there's far more effort put into it in this government than there's ever been before, certainly than there ever was when I was first in government.

Ah, those lost days of grand, high policy-making. Perhaps rather surprisingly a more modern politician, Peter Walker, the Minister of Agriculture, also thinks that management is a diversion of the politician's true talents.

Walker:

Can I point out that one of the great snags of dealing with this problem by the politician is that the politician is not by character or training a man-manager in terms of administration. You know, if you take some of our most popular politicians in history, like Winston Churchill and William

1 Lord Soames was Leader of the House of Lords and Minister for the Civil Service from 1979–81. He lost the job three months after this programme was broadcast in the Cabinet reshuffle of 14 September 1981.

> Pitt, the great names of British history, you wouldn't actually bring them in to run an office. It wasn't their sort of greatness. Their greatness was political strategy and a sense of history and a sense of what the world was all about, and that's what the politician is there for. When I was at the Department of the Environment I had, I think, a staff of 78,000, all of whom knew that they would be there a lot longer than I would; it's not the ideal relationship to go in and streamline the department and get it better organised.

All of which will come as a surprise to one of Peter Walker's successors at the Department of the Environment, the present Secretary of State, Michael Heseltine. He would entirely refute the thesis that politicians can't be managers, can't themselves do much about cutting the size of the service. Mr Heseltine is Rayner Man incarnate. As soon as he got to his immense, sprawling department in May 1979, he started up something called MINIS, a Management Information System,[1] which exposed a pretty fundamental question.

Heseltine:

> It is designed to put in front of ministers the totality of what is happening in this department. And, broadly, what we did in the early stages was to get the senior civil servants – there were about sixty-six in charge of divisions – to analyse down to the nearest thousand pounds what each of their staff was doing in the course of a period. It's very fascinating that no one had ever asked anyone to do that before. But once it was done, it meant that ministers were able to look to see exactly what was happening in the area for which they were responsible. It enabled those sixty-six civil servants in charge of divisions to look to see what their immediate subordinates and ultimate subordinates were doing. The interesting thing, one rapidly discovered, was that no such information existed. There was no way when I came here in which anyone could actually answer the question, 'What are the civil servants in this department doing?'

One of the things this exercise threw up was precisely the problem Sir Derek Rayner mentioned: that although civil servants are good at abiding by the rules, these rules, and espe-

1 MINIS Report 1, November 1980. MINIS Report 2, July 1981.

cially the monitoring of everyone by somebody else, are a dubious extravagance.

Heseltine:

First of all, there was the double banking of the administrative grades by the professional grades. If you had a particular problem, whether in pollution or in land policy or whatever, you wouldn't have a chap who had the particular skills heading a department to deal with that. You tended to have an administrator, and he would have an equivalent group of people with professional skills advising him. That, of course, gave you more people than you needed and so we amalgamated those and generally put either the administrator or the chap with the professional skills in charge of one group of people dealing specifically with that problem.

There have also been concrete, measurable, identifiable cuts.

Heseltine:

We wound up a Planning Intelligence Division, because we reckoned that the other existing divisions in the planning field were perfectly capable of having their own intelligence appraisal of the situation without another double-banking process alongside them. We've made very similar economies in the research field where we reckoned that the specialist divisions knew enough about their own requirements to determine their own research objectives without having a research division trying to double-guess their activities. The statistical divisions have been very much reduced where, again, you had specialist divisions collecting the information for the expert administrative divisions. A lot of the overseas work, where people were going off to committees and endless discussions of various international bodies, has gone. One just didn't see a pay-off for the British people from that sort of activity.

All this does, however, have its costs. It's built on a fairly crude kind of political will. Assembling the political will does undoubtedly involve the generation of hostility towards civil servants as a class. Dedicated public officials like Mike Fogden, seconded to Newcastle, are almost, but not completely, stoical about this.

Fogden:

I suppose it does have a slightly wearing effect in the background but I think when you enter the service, you

> recognise that you're probably entering an area of public infamy, inasmuch as we're rated alongside mothers-in-law and Wigan Pier and other funny aspects of society that are tolerated but not necessarily accepted. What it is sometimes difficult to come to terms with is if it's manifestly overt that any one administration is not particularly sympathetic to the servants that work for it.

Nor, as Labour politician and former minister Roy Hattersley fairly says, is public service simply a matter of efficiency.

> *Hattersley*:
>
> I think the attack on the bureaucracy, which is made by the Conservative government, is philosophically very much related to all the clichés about rolling back the frontiers of the state. If you don't build any council houses, then you don't need any civil servants to administer the grants that go towards building council houses. If you actually reduce the quality and provision of the health service, then you need less people in the Department of Health and Social Security. I think the two things emotionally and philosophically very much go together in the Tory mind. It may be that in a marginal way the Labour party was less diligent in avoiding the recruitment of the extra hundred, extra fifty, extra 500 civil servants, but I think our view on the civil service was a much more rational one than theirs, which is that you've got to perform a number of tasks and you have to have the people to perform them. I think one of the more unpleasant features of the Tory attitude over the last two years has been their calculated attack on the civil service. It's had an enormous effect on civil service morale, which is very low, and it's had an enormous effect on civil service performance as a result. I believe successive governments are going to have to do a great deal of work to get the civil service back into condition, both in terms of numbers and in terms of morale.

The big pay-off from the Thatcher years, in this respect, should be elsewhere. Civil servants may be unpopular, and their morale may not be what it was. The top ones, however, certainly say they are more conscious of efficiency and are far better attuned to improving it. But this, one has to say, is not the opinion of Sir Derek Rayner. Maybe he sets impossibly high standards. But on the question of whether the attitude of senior civil servants towards managerial efficiency has really changed, under the whip of Thatcherism and indeed Raynerism, he was disappointed.

> *Rayner*:
>
> Taken as a whole, I must be frank and say, 'No'. There are a number of senior civil servants who are very much aware of the needs of management, so it's not an overall criticism, but the answer is, 'No, it's not developed along the lines that I would have imagined it would.'

But all is not quite lost.

> *Rayner*:
>
> What has changed, however, is the range of skills that are being recruited. My memory may serve me false, but in 1970 many of the younger people at Principal level came from the conventional background of a university with degrees in traditional subjects. Today I find many of them come from a wide range of science and engineering backgrounds, so the recruitment itself seems to have improved to bring in a broader range of disciplines.

And to this ground we turn next. Who does get into the civil service? Who gets promoted and why? Twenty years ago one was brought up to think that civil servants really were the highest fliers of our time: imaginative, brilliantly clever, impenetrably adept manipulators of power. After seeing more of them, it becomes quite clear that this picture is wrong. They have other qualities – but are they the right ones?

Civil Servants are Incompetent

First Broadcast: 28 June 1981

The senior civil service is a self-perpetuating élite. It decides who shall be admitted to its number at the bottom level. It also decides who shall rise to the top. Politicians have almost nothing to do with this process even though they are held responsible for the results. Over only a minute number of jobs at the very top do ministers occasionally exert a power of choice. And, even then, they are usually limited to a field of about three candidates who are deemed by the heads of the Service to be eligible for the next vacant Permanent Secretaryship. It is therefore of some considerable interest to know what human qualities find most favour with the mandarins who appoint their successors – usually, as with so many professions, in their own image: men – and it is almost always men still – like Sir Donald Maitland, Permanent Secretary at the Department of Energy.

Maitland:

Oral expression, written expression, judgement, ability to get on with people – these are some of the basic skills. After all, most civil servants' work is written: they take part in meetings; they have to defend a case; they have to argue against a case; so advocacy, whether on paper or orally, is one of the basic skills of the civil servant. Getting on with people – there's no point in being a brilliant advocate if you antagonise people from the word 'go'. But above all, sound judgement and the ability to learn.

To these professional skills, says Patrick Nairne, Permanent Secretary at the Department of Health and Social Security,[1] must be added what one might call the human dimension.

Nairne:

He does need to be good intellectually but he wouldn't be here if he wasn't. I'm looking, I think, primarily at his character and personality. I do, of course, get to know all the young entrants into my department, in the sense that I myself have a talk with them alone after they've been six months with the department and I then see them again

1 Sir Patrick Nairne retired as Permanent Secretary in July 1981.

roughly when their probation period is over. We often talk about this, because I do think that the young are obsessed with getting through intellectual exams and they have been since they were at school. What I try to get over to them is that being an effective civil servant means delivering the goods. It's not just writing things down on bits of paper; it's not the job of a sort of don manqué, it is actually getting things done. And getting things done usually means persuading other people to do it, or getting tasks completed in co-operation with others. Sometimes when they don't want to do it, you've got to persuade them. So I'm very much looking for those who've got the right character and personality combined with the intellect for the task.

In the Home Office, it seems, they worry very much about getting things done. Sir Brian Cubbon is the Permanent Secretary there.

Cubbon:

A mixture of character, general ability, particular talents, particular record, certainly appetite for the work, certainly high intelligence, political nose. An ability to get on with people. An ability to negotiate and advocate particular courses of action. Someone who also worries a little perhaps. I like to feel that one or two members of the Home Office actually cut themselves shaving in the morning while thinking about some problem.

In the Civil Service Department itself,[1] however, such nervous anxiety is less highly regarded than something rather more mundane, as Sir Ian Bancroft explains.

Bancroft:

I could be very tripping-off-the-tongue here. I could say, you need energy; you need intelligence; you need integrity; you need ability to manage resources, both human and the rest. But you need something else, I think. You need, amongst other things, this mysterious thing called discretion. By that I don't mean a grey timidity. What I mean is that you are the guardians of an awful lot of information between yourselves and ministers, and between yourselves and the public – many of whose private lives are displayed on files – and between yourselves and companies with their

1 *See* footnote 1 on p. 22.

> commercial secrets. Therefore, if you're going to carry the confidence of all the clientele, you have got to be, and be seen to be, discreet in the best sense of the word.

Most of the qualities listed by these four distinguished gentlemen as being necessary for anyone who aspires to follow them to the top of Whitehall's greasy pole have one feature in common. They are, by and large, conservative qualities. Discretion, judgement, civility, fluency – these are sober, even boring virtues. And since we are about to cast a little doubt on what Whitehall regards most highly, let Peter Walker, the Minister of Agriculture, remind us of another which should not be forgotten.

> *Walker*:
>
> I think another important thing about the civil service tradition, which we always forget in this country because it's taken for granted, is that it is, unbelievably by world standards, free of corruption. I always recall when I was Secretary of State for the Environment, where I was involved in making planning decisions which made fortunes for people or lost fortunes for people, that there was a group of civil servants called 'inspectors' who carried out these great public inquiries where they made decisions with enormous consequences, and there was never a case involving any accusation or suggestion of corruption at all. Now that is a unique position in terms of modern government worldwide and a terrific prize, actually. It means that you have a civil service that has this high integrity, and in governing a country I think that's an enormous advantage.

It's an advantage certainly, but are integrity and all these associated qualities really enough? Can we really be satisfied with a civil service primarily dedicated to keeping the show on the road? Taking no risks; composing well-balanced briefs; making sure that ministers aren't embarrassed? One man who has unusual authority for doubting it is William Plowden. He had one of the most varied and meteoric careers in Whitehall as a young man, and he's still not very old. But he got out in order to be free and he's now running the Royal Institute of Public Administration, much revitalised under his direction. Originality, now much neglected, is a virtue which he would add to the list.

> *Plowden*:
>
> I think my ideally good civil servant would be looking for new ways of making organisations operate, for totally new

> ways round problems. He'd be trying to find solutions to problems which might not necessarily commend themselves to his ministers but which would be worth putting forward because they'd be different and have some chance of succeeding. I think what's required is a feeling of pressing up against, and perhaps beyond, the boundaries of the possible. It is the notion of creativity that seems to be lacking. One doesn't want civil servants to take the lead necessarily in politics; it isn't their job. But one wants them to believe that novelty is possible, and also that novelty will be acceptable to politicians if it can be sold to them.

Another man with extensive Whitehall experience, but who also enjoys the refreshment of regular escapes into another world, is Professor Brian Abel-Smith of the London School of Economics. He's worked for several Labour governments as a special adviser at the DHSS where, it appears, they sometimes weren't even much good at writing.

Abel-Smith:

> I wouldn't have looked for the qualities for promotion which on average I found around me when I was in departments. The type of chap who wants to thrust through a policy, has ideas, wants to be creative, wants to change things, tends not to get pushed forward. There are also parallel skills needed – to be able to write, to be able to write a good Cabinet memo, to be able to write a speech. It is an unusual combination in civil servants – some are extremely good at thinking up policies but are terribly dreary on paper, which may be all right for other civil servants to read but hopeless for a speech or Cabinet. When you find a man with this combination I would say he's the sort of man I would like to see promoted. But I think they go for the good Whitehall man – the man who is liked by other departments, doesn't rock the boat, is very charming, makes his points very gently, unemotionally, sees all sides of every question – an all-round type of chap, which doesn't lead to dynamic leadership.

Of this species there could be no more shining example than the Permanent Secretary at the Ministry of Agriculture, Sir Brian Hayes. Sir Brian is something of a phenomenon in Whitehall. He was still a mere Assistant Secretary, the fourth rung down, at the age of thirty-eight, yet had risen to the very top before he was fifty. But before we try to pin down what exactly it was that made him so brilliant, a story from one of his colleagues is worth telling. It concerns some all-night negotiation over the EEC agriculture policy in Brussels. There was Sir Brian, conducting this very sticky haggle for Britain, and when it broke up at 4.00 am, his assistants said that they would set about drafting the telegram to be sent back to London. 'Oh, I've done that,' said Sir Brian, producing it out of his hip pocket. Well then, they'd prepare the parliamentary statement, they said. 'I've actually done that as well,' Sir Brian said, almost apologetically. Thus, drafting several statements at once and faster than a typist can keep up, while negotiating and listening to multi-lingual translation, seems to define at least one kind of Whitehall excellence. Who better, then, than Sir Brian Hayes to epitomise in one lethal definition the middle-minded all-rounder that Brian Abel-Smith was talking about.

Hayes:

I suspect not many eccentrics apply to join the civil service unless you think we all have to be eccentric to want to work in it. In practice the true eccentric, which I would define as someone who has very strong views on particular issues, would not fit easily into the civil service context. The civil service only works well if it is politically neutral. It cannot be if it includes people with extremely strong political or other views which relate to policy. And your eccentric might very well fit into that category.

Oddly enough, that's not something all ministers would agree with. In our conversations we've become accustomed to the pretty respectful view which most politicians take of civil servants: reliability above every other virtue. Shirley Williams, however, conjured up a whole new picture.

Williams:

The civil service is rather better than many other promotion structures in allowing the slightly heterodox or unconventional man or woman to move up. I had one civil servant, for example, who always insisted on coming to the department – she was a very senior civil servant – in pretty ropey jeans and made no concession at all, not even the slightest one, to the normal conventions of civil service behaviour. I had another civil servant who was given to pop music and fairly heavy drinking, but nevertheless was a very able man. As a consequence of living a fairly free life, he used to break out into the most vituperative attacks on what I

> was putting forward as a minister, with no concessions whatsoever to politeness and none of this 'Secretary of State' business and so on. He was very blunt indeed. Yet he has been steadily promoted, and rightly so, because he's an extremely brilliant, unusual and creative man.

What Mrs Williams described is certainly unusual, but the real question is whether the more typical top civil servant is precisely the kind of person the country needs. Does he have the right skills? What the Permanent Secretaries describe adds up to a skilful pure administrator, a paper-pusher and dis-embarrasser of ministers. But the tests such men have to pass, as the Secretary of State for the Environment, Michael Heseltine, suggests, are much more elusive than those faced by, say, an industrialist.

> *Heseltine*:
> The industrialist is a man who has to make quick decisions. He has very simple objectives in the main, which are to earn a return on the assets employed. He has standards of performance which are clear. He has a measurement of his success which is on a regular basis and which tends to be capable of being added up at the end of the month or the week or whatever it may be. He's a man who's going to have to take quicker decisions. He's a man who's often going to have to take more risky decisions. There's a very considerable element of winner takes all. He's also usually part of a much more united team because they all work for the same company, they're all going to be there a long time, they all tend to be specialists in their own field contributing to the whole. Now all of those qualities are very different from what one needs and expects in the civil service. Here you have a system where you come in as a minister with a set of policies, expecting the co-operation of a group of people who have a sense of looking after the machinery of government permanently. They are cautious people because in public administration the degree of criticism for failure is enormous, and the credit for success a great deal less.

Sir Ian Bancroft is not unaware of this distinction.

> *Bancroft*:
> We also have the question of motivation. In many organisations you have one single motivator which is profit, and that in turn, of course, depends on giving satisfaction to

> the consumer. But in the civil service you have to be aware of the fact that the government of the day, any government of the day, is pursuing like fun a whole variety of different objectives. You've got to be aware of those, especially when they're in conflict with one another. And still on the subject of motivation, quite often, if one is advising on policy, there's nothing concrete at the end of the day to see as a result of several years' effort. So I think that one also needs mental and physical toughness in adversity.

Other civil servants, like Patrick Nairne, see caution not as a convenient alibi but as the inescapable result of parliamentary democracy.

Nairne:

> It is true that the nature of the system in which civil servants work is one that does tend to promote caution and conservatism. I think the reasons for this are very well known. There is the constant battering, and rightly so, by Parliament on the executive. If you are constantly concerned with the parliamentary questions that are coming up, and with the enormous spate of letters, and we get thousands of letters, a rising number of letters every year from Members of Parliament; and if ministers are very properly sensitive to the need to avoid being exposed to unnecessary embarrassment when questioned about things that have not yet been fully worked out, then I think it is inevitable that a system like that, which has the immense advantage of ministers being questioned in the House, inevitably also carries the potential disadvantage that those who serve ministers will tend to be somewhat on the defensive and rather cautious and conservative.

In other words, avoiding blunders is at least as important as delivering results. There's a real tension here. But together with the high value Whitehall places on the sheer status of, for example, being in a minister's private office as a major qualification for future and greater status, this priority is hard for a true businessman to understand. Sir Derek Rayner was brought in by Margaret Thatcher to inculcate business standards of efficiency into Whitehall.[1] He's pretty exasperated by the contrast

1 Sir Derek Rayner, Joint Managing Director of Marks & Spencer, was appointed in 1979 to act on a part-time basis as adviser to the Prime Minister on improving efficiency and eliminating waste in government. He had had two previous secondments to government (*see* p. 18).

between the gilded path to the top of the government and the stony obstacle-course to success in business.

> *Rayner*:
>
> The civil servant naturally observes what is the most likely road to promotion and he will observe, certainly from the past, that periods in private office and in policy work are more likely to lead to the top than running a large block of work such as a local office or a regional office. This has changed somewhat in the last two years, but I think that change will have to continue for some time before it is recognised that the route to the top is actually to run something rather than think about something.

Also, he thinks, there's a shortage of basic technical skills.

> *Rayner*:
>
> The other problem is their inability to attract the right kinds of, for example, financial management. These people are, of course, highly paid outside and there they clearly can see a road to the top because there are not many boards of directors that do not contain at least one person from that background, but there are many ministries where the top echelon contains not a single person with such a background. So again until it is seen that accountants can move to the top, and I mean accountants in the broad financial-management sense, there will be a problem in attracting the right kind of skills. Attempts, serious attempts, have been made to do so but, in my opinion, so far they have not attracted the numbers which they need.

To which Peter Walker, himself a now somewhat ageing whizz kid from the financial world,[1] has one answer – and also a cautionary tale.

> *Walker*:
>
> If you're going to tackle that from within the civil service, you've got to retain people of the ability of the Derek Rayners of this world, and you've got to pay them the Derek Rayner sort of salaries of this world. And you can't have it both ways. I remember some time ago when the Treasury used to experiment by releasing bright young men from the Treasury to the merchant banks, and the merchant banks produced bright young men to go to the Treasury.

1 Peter Walker is reputed to have made his first million by the age of twenty-seven.

> What happened was that all the bright young men from the merchant banks went back to the merchant banks, and all the bright young men from the Treasury stayed with the merchant banks, and there was a net loss because the bright young men found there were better terms and better conditions, more freedom and perhaps less frustration than in their considerable careers in the civil service.

It is the contention of civil servants that while they may be deficient in that sort of competence, other sorts of specialist now abound, in breeds and degrees an earlier generation would have found unthinkable. At the Department of Energy, Sir Donald Maitland handed over a list, written in his own neat italic hand, of the kind of specialists now occupying important positions in his department. One-third of the Assistant Secretaries, it showed, are mathematicians, actuaries, bio-physicists, chemists and the like. One-third of the Principals, a rank below, are engineers and aerodynamicists. Besides, the mandarins heatedly deny that merely because a man is a generalist – a pure administrator, the kind who gets right to the top – he doesn't have to deliver results and subject himself to rigorous assessment. This, they say, is achieved by the annual 'confidential report', an enormously elaborate surveillance system, by which officials appraise the work and prospects of people below them and then, of course, are themselves appraised by people above them. Upon this edifice of quality control sits proudly at the peak the head of the Service, Sir Ian Bancroft.

These report forms aren't easy to come by, even when they're blank. But happily someone slipped us a copy. No fewer than nine pages have to be filled in. At the heart of them is a checklist enumerating fifteen desirable qualities: foresight, judgement, penetration, our old friends oral and written expression, and so on. For each, a helpful scale of grading is supplied. Thus virtue number 11, 'reliability under pressure', ranges from 'unflustered, competent, reliable at all times' which scores A, to 'easily thrown off balance, not reliable, even under normal pressure', an F or zero score. Not everyone is quite so enchanted as the mandarins with this arrangement. From Barney Hayhoe, the junior minister for the civil service,[1] one gets just a whiff of the weakness of a closed assessment system.

1 When the Civil Service Department was abolished on 12 November 1981 Barney Hayhoe, whilst continuing to be responsible for civil service affairs, became Minister of State at the Treasury.

Hayhoe:
I do believe that there has been a tendency over the years for the people in charge of those more junior to them not always to report wholly fairly and honestly about them, in other words to be kind. And sometimes their kindness is perhaps even damaging to the career prospects of the people beneath them, who may not be performing well in one job but would do jolly well if they were transferred to work that they were better able to do. Our reporting systems, our methods of assessing the quality of people, do, I think, need improvement, and I hope that improvement is taking place.

Improved or not, and accurate or not, what is integral to this system is one conspicuous danger: it is likely to be more than usually hard to skip fast up the hierarchy. Such remorselessly systematic assessment usually leads to equally measured and systematic promotion. Even the proverbial Whitehall high-flier tends to reach the heights only latish in life, after everyone else has been passed dutifully through ahead of him. According to Denis Healey, this can often be too late.

Healey:
My own view is that the average level of competence in the civil service is much higher than in other walks of life, and perhaps higher than is required in the civil service, given the weaknesses in other areas of British life. I think you'll find that almost any businessman, if you take one example, who's gone to work with the civil service on a short-term basis, starts off by being staggered at the brilliance of most of the people he's working with. It's by no means universal, and I think there is a tendency for civil servants to work so hard up to the age of fifty or fifty-five that they tend to tread water or be burnt out for their last five years.

And fifty-five is a dangerous age for that to happen. Just the kind of mark around which the average top mandarin is finally promoted to run his department. By this time, William Plowden says, with the grim detachment of a man who saw what was coming and got out, creativity has been squeezed out of him, whatever other virtues remain.

Plowden:
I think several things are squeezed out of them. First, there's the effect of the sheer passage of time. By the time you get to your middle or late fifties at any level in any

> organisation much of your youthful fire will tend to have gone, unless you're a pretty unusual person. The other thing that happens to them is that, if they're any good, they are ruthlessly exploited in the earlier stages of their careers. They find it very difficult to get time off to think. The best people are used again and again in the key jobs, the places where jobs are under pressure, and they can, I think, generally lose the capacity for thought in the fullest sense of the term.

Brian Abel-Smith, from his privileged viewpoint inside and yet outside the ministry as a special adviser, puts it a lot less delicately.

> *Abel-Smith*:
> I also see an element which I thought was rather destructive: Buggins' turn. Here's the more senior chap, poor chap, we don't want to overlook him, we know he's a bit deadbeat – I wonder if they do actually know that he's a bit deadbeat – but I think he's a bit deadbeat. Perhaps he was very good when he was younger but lost the great drive and enthusiasm he might have had then. And here's this chap going up to a pretty giddy height. Meanwhile, I can see whizz kids two levels below. If I was making the appointment I'd have given the senior job to the whizz kid aged thirty-five. I'd have promoted youngsters.

Professor Abel-Smith compares civil service life with the academic world: just as many dull, dreary dons as dull, dreary officials. But he also insists that there are these whizz kids whom he, as a special adviser, reckons he valued a lot higher than some Permanent Secretaries did.

> *Abel-Smith*:
> Marvellous people. Dynamic, thrusting. In fact a lot of the job of a special adviser, once you get known within a department, is to know whom to ring. I mean you ring number three and not number one. Or you deal always with number two because number one is an absolute drear and it takes hours to explain anything to him, and anyway you find obstruction. And you ring number two and he says, 'Yes, we'll get on with it. We'll do it.'

Some politicians are not so mesmerised by the service Whitehall offers as to be blind to the force of this. The assessment system may grind its way forward, throwing up the sober, steady, hard-working types who now run the service. But Peter Walker, for one, finds the anomalies of public life distinctly jarring.

Walker:

I've always held the view that it's crazy that you can become a Cabinet minister in your thirties, that you can become the head of a great business house in your twenties,[1] that you have a dazzling career in the private sector in your twenties and early thirties, but it's virtually impossible to do so in the civil service. The civil servant, the traditional civil servant, will argue that on reflection the accumulated experience he's gathered before he's reached the dizzy heights of Permanent Secretary gives him a maturity of wisdom which is of great benefit. I concede that argument. But personally I would go for a system whereby the really bright able person could quickly go through to the top.

As ever, Whitehall has an answer to this. We've found in the last few months that it has an answer, sometimes more than one, to almost everything. It's supplied here by Sir Ian Bancroft. First, there are the exceptions that disprove the rule that all Permanent Secretaries are between fifty-five and sixty.

Bancroft:

Well, that's untrue for a start. There are some who were promoted in their late forties and are just knocking over fifty.[2] The notion of the slow tramp up the promotion ladder is just not true. We can, and do, have accelerated promotions. One doesn't want to be too anecdotal but I know of two Under-Secretaries who were promoted at the age of thirty-eight, and one of the young men that I've just been talking to on another subject became an Assistant Secretary at the age of thirty-three.

And then, perhaps, there's a more general rule, which suggests that Mr Buggins – later, God willing, to become Sir Humphrey Buggins – must indeed have his turn.

Bancroft:

Of course one's got to have some general pattern, otherwise the able characters, not absolute fliers but the able charac-

1 Peter Walker himself became Chairman of a firm of Lloyds Brokers at the age of twenty-six and a Cabinet minister at thirty-eight.

2 In September 1981, a few months after this programme was broadcast, the appointment of Sir Anthony Acland to succeed Sir Michael Palliser as Permanent Secretary to the Foreign and Commonwealth Office was announced. He was fifty-one.

ters, who ought to be able to expect a reasonable career in the service, would constantly get overtaken by the young fliers. And what happens to the young fliers, if they're promoted to Permanent Secretary at the age of thirty-five or thereabouts, when they've been in posts for ten years and they're still only forty-five?

All of which gives rise to the perverse thought that just possibly there are too many capable people in the civil service whose competence lies in unproductive directions and whom the system encourages towards that caricature which may be all too near the truth – of a massive paper-circulating factory employing too many people who actually do, and take responsiblity for, very little. William Plowden paints the dreadful picture.

Plowden:

I think you can sense it in the civil service by simply sitting at your desk in a middle or senior position and looking bemused at the enormous wodges of photocopied documents that are put on your desk daily from people in other bits of the same department or other departments saying, 'You might possibly have a view on this? Can you comment?' In most cases you probably don't and can't, but the perennial need of the civil servant to check that everybody's happy is now exacerbated by the invention of the photocopier. I think there are too many senior people in the civil service, period. That's to say there are too many people cutting each job into smaller and finer pieces and climbing over each other's backs and looking at each other's drafts and generally getting in each other's way, and they're very good at doing this. I think the job would be more satisfying and would probably be better done if there was more scope for the individual to operate, to take decisions, to be responsible for a larger block of work, as indeed it used to be fifteen or twenty or fifty years ago.

But what exactly is 'responsibility' in the context of a profession which in the end can always, with sound constitutional authority, offload the blame on to ministers? Are civil servants being made by Parliament to be more personally accountable? More profoundly, are they in any way responsible for the state of Britain today? The text book says No. But what, when pressed, do *they* say?

Civil Servants are Unaccountable

First broadcast: 5 July 1981

As every citizen knows, the hardest thing to bear about any contact with the government, whether it's the local social security office at one end of the scale or the collapsing economy at the other, is the difficulty of finding out who exactly is in charge. Who's ultimately to blame? Passing the buck is not merely a skill to be cultivated by any sensible bureaucrat. It is, at one level, positively ordained by the constitutional textbooks. Civil servants say they are not, in the end, to be held responsible for decisions. They merely carry out the will of ministers. Therefore, wherever the buck stops, it does not stop with them.

But this pure model of the constitution is plainly unsatisfactory. It suggests that the working environment of the civil service is a kind of moral vacuum, where no sanctions exist and no named person is to be held accountable for anything he does. This is quite clearly nonsense. Yet, picking our way towards the truth about how, and why, and to what extent civil servants feel and are held responsible for what they say and do, takes us on an elusive path. At the top, accountability in the most obvious sense is to be seen in action in the House of Commons' most powerful committee: the Public Accounts Committee. This is where a check is kept on the billions of pounds for which Permanent Secretaries have to account. The committee is served by its own mini-bureaucracy and invariably chaired by a former Cabinet minister from the opposition: at present Joel Barnett, Chief Secretary to the Treasury in the Callaghan government.

Barnett:

We have the Comptroller and Auditor General and his staff of approximately 600 working effectively to prepare reports on which we base our work. Those reports are audit-based: that is, they are based on a financial audit of departments and other public bodies, so that during the course of those financial audits they throw up not just whether the figures add up or not, but whether there has been value for money; whether there has been inefficiency in the management of public funds; whether there are better ways of managing a particular budget; whether the original estimate for, let us say, a project of £100 million that has turned out to be costing £300 million after ten years, or five years, or four years or whatever, is reasonable or is due to things beyond the control of the department or to ministerial decisions that changed the project out of all recognition, or whether it's due to pure incompetence or, in some cases, to fraud.

The grilling which takes place on the basis of these reports, always highlighting what went wrong rather than what went right, is an inescapable part of every Permanent Secretary's year, for which all of them, like Sir Brian Hayes at the Ministry of Agriculture, prepare meticulously.

Hayes:

It does involve a lot of work because one never knows what questions will be asked and one therefore has to brief oneself absolutely thoroughly on every aspect of the question the PAC are looking into, so that one can answer any question. That does mean quite a lot of evenings of concentration and effort and memorising before one goes to give evidence.

Perhaps he even enjoyed this kind of public performance?

Hayes:

Yes, strangely enough I do. I didn't at first. The first two or three times I appeared before the Public Accounts Committee I was petrified, but nowadays I'm enjoying it more. I also think it is a very valuable part of the constitutional process in this country. I'm very much in favour of open government myself and I like the opportunity to explain why we do what we do.

For Sir Patrick Nairne, head of the DHSS,[1] the nature of the accountability going on here must be precisely, almost pedantically, defined.

Nairne:

I'm accountable, not to the Public Accounts Committee, but to my Secretary of State. I am answerable to the Public Accounts Committee, however, in this sense: that I have to sign the accounts for the National Health Service vote, for the administration vote of the department. The

---

1 Sir Patrick Nairne retired as Permanent Secretary in July 1981 and when we interviewed him in May 1981 he had just completed his final series of appearances before the PAC.

> Comptroller and Auditor General reports on those accounts to the PAC, so I am required to be the principal witness for the department. And I do feel that this is a responsibility of a very personal kind.

Nor is it just before the committee that he sees himself as being on trial.

> *Nairne*:
>
> I may say that I feel that my authority would be very much weakened in the department if I didn't do that job well. There is, to be honest, a kind of gladiatorial element about it that I think is rather a strain for an accounting officer and a Permanent Secretary. I think it's of value to the department generally because there is a great deal of work in preparing for it and that does mean that when matters have been the subject of criticism, those criticisms are discussed very fully within the department, going down to quite a low level. And, of course, in respect of the National Health Service, going into the NHS as well.

Rather less personal but just as important to this question of civil servants' responsibility are the hearings of select committees in the House of Commons. The Public Accounts Committee is essentially an auditor of the past. Select committees convene to inquire into the present and future, usually with a view to commenting on policy and making recommendations. One of the purposes seen for them, at least by the most zealous of their proponents, is precisely this capacity to summon and interrogate civil servants, bringing them out of the woodwork. The committees have grown in number and power in recent years, especially under the present government, and now they're all the rage – although, as Sir Ian Bancroft says, selecting one of the most familiar of Whitehall's crushing rejoinders, they're in fact not exactly new.

> *Bancroft*:
>
> I'm told, though I've not read the particular extract from his diary, that Pepys records with great pride an appearance before a select committee to do with the Navy.[1] The PAC, Public Accounts Committee, has been with us for donkey's years.[2] We had the Crossman experiments in the

1 In his *Diary* of 22 October 1667 Samuel Pepys gives an account of his evidence, as Head of the Navy Office, to the Committee of Miscarriages, and in the entry for 5 March 1668 of his evidence to a Committee of the whole House.

2 It was established in 1862.

late sixties.[1] We had the Expenditure Committee in the seventies.[2] The difference between the former select committees and the present ones is that these, on the whole, are departmentally related; they cover nearly all the departments[3] and they're appointed for the life of the Parliament and not just for the session. I think they're rather a good thing.

So do a lot of other people, especially at Westminster. However, as with any interrogation or dialogue, the success of select committees depends on the ability of MPs to ask the right questions and the willingness of civil servants to answer them: neither of which can be absolutely relied on. For one thing, civil servants are quite determined not to get drawn into discussing policy questions or 'who gave what advice to whom' on any particular issue. This limitation need not always be an impediment to effectiveness. Edward du Cann, the Conservative MP who chairs the select committee on Treasury and Civil Service Affairs, considers his committee scored a bullseye in its recent inquiry into monetarism.[4]

Du Cann:

I wouldn't ask a civil servant to defend monetarism as a sole method of economic policy, but what I would ask a civil servant to do is to justify, for example, the assumptions underlying the medium-term economic forecast. I'll give you a precise example of what I mean. In the original medium-term economic forecast there was a series of figures, a series of assumptions. One of them was for the turn-round, the proposed turn-round, the assumed turn-

1 Under the 'Crossman Reforms' of 1966 specialist select committees to consider either a subject area, e.g. Race Relations and Immigration, or a Department, e.g. Education and Science, were established. They were appointed for each session for the duration of a Parliament until 1979.

2 The Expenditure Committee, whose terms of reference were to consider how, if at all, the policies implied in the figures of expenditure and in the estimates may be carried out more economically, lasted from 1971–9. The Committee's work was carried out through six largely autonomous sub-committees: Trade and Industry; Education, Arts and Home Office; General; Defence and External Affairs; Environment; Employment and Social Services.

3 The new select committee structure was established in June 1979. There are fourteen such departmental committees: Agriculture; Defence; Education, Science and Arts; Employment; Energy; Environment; Foreign Affairs; Home Affairs; Industry and Trade; Scottish Affairs; Social Services; Transport; Treasury and Civil Service; Welsh Affairs.

4 House Of Commons *Third Report from the Treasury and Civil Service Committee*, Session 1980–81, *Monetary Policy*, 3 Vols, HC163, HMSO, 1981.

round, in the affairs of the nationalised industries; that represented a swing of two and a half billion pounds. So we could ask the Chancellor how he came to set the medium-term economic strategy, what he thought it would achieve and the rest of it. When it came to civil servants, we would say, 'Where are the figures which justify this particular assumption?' And as the world now knows, the figures simply weren't there. In other words, if you want to attend to the nuts and bolts, and some of those nuts and bolts are so significant that the machine would fall apart without them, then you go to the civil servants.

Mr du Cann has little fault to find with the civil servants who appear before his committee. They are, he says, very co-operative. But take something much more down to earth than monetarism. The select committee on Social Services held an inquiry into perinatal and neonatal mortality – the death of babies at or just after birth.[1] The committee found what it regarded as a scandalous state of affairs for late twentieth-century Britain and said that 5000 lives might be saved if enough money was spent on the relevant services. This was not what the DHSS wanted to hear. Tim Nodder, the Deputy Secretary in charge of this particular piece of work, supervised the assembling of a massive brief for the committee: one which scarcely echoed its own burning sense of discovery.

Nodder:

I think that one of the first things we were able to establish with the committee, I hope successfully, was that they had picked on a subject to which a good deal of attention had been given, not only in the department but elsewhere, and we were able to explain to them one or two initiatives which ministers had taken which were having some effect.

And when it came to the oral hearing?

Nodder:

There's a certain tenseness. To some degree one is faced with something rather like an examination for which one has prepared in depth. There's always a risk of making a gaffe. The obvious one is, of course, not having the right information or giving the wrong information. More important, I think, is the risk that there will be some misun-

1 House of Commons *Second Report from the Social Services Committee*, Session 1979–80, *Perinatal and Neonatal Mortality*, Vol. 1, HC663–1, HMSO, 1980.

derstanding or misconception created which, once it's established in the minds of people in this rather adversarial context, is difficult to get away from. This can cause difficulty.

But it's more than a question of causing misunderstandings or not having the right information. When they appear before these committees, civil servants are under instruction to observe a code of conduct, laid down by the Civil Service Department, that decrees what – and far more urgently, what *not* – to say. In particular, they must say nothing about personalities or internal disagreements in the department: the truth and nothing but the truth, but certainly not the whole truth. According to one committee chairman, Christopher Price, the Labour MP who chairs the Select Committee on Education, this causes civil servants extensive and unnecessary toil.

Price:

The extra burden that it puts on them is sometimes feeling that they must rewrite every piece of paper especially for the select committee. We have powers to send for persons and papers but they never send us an original document. They 'massage' it for the select committee. I was at a conference recently with a very senior civil servant from the Civil Service Department, and I was complaining about this cosmetic process and saying, 'Look, if you didn't do that and just gave us the documents, it would save you an awful lot of time and public money. Couldn't you just xerox things?' And he said, 'Oh, don't worry, Mr Price, we do it for ministers also. We rewrite everything.' And my view is that one could save an awful lot of money in Whitehall if, as is the case to a certain extent now in the United States, civil servants just xeroxed things for committees instead of getting some little boy to rewrite the whole thing and then sending the whole paper up to the Permanent Secretary until it's finally okayed for select committees.

Equally, one must remember that there are civil servants, and for that matter politicians, who contend that the committee process is sometimes thwarted by the way MPs play it: the incompetence (dare one put such a word into the mouth of a mandarin?) with which they ask the questions – even, says Sir Patrick Nairne, in the great Public Accounts Committee.

Nairne:

Let me say at once that the chairman of the Public Accounts

> Committee is exceedingly well briefed and, as he is an ex-minister from the Treasury, he is exceedingly shrewd and exacting in his questions. And the other members of the PAC are, for the most part, very experienced. A large number of them have been members throughout the period of my appearances in the last six years and are very good at knowing what kind of questions will probe an accounting officer best. But having said that, yes, I do sometimes feel that I'm being asked a question and expected to give an answer in two or three lines, when it really needs a careful memorandum of about ten pages, followed by half a dozen questions probably composed by me, as being the best questions they ought to be asking me.

The question one keeps asking, the more one looks into this process, is: what exactly is going on here? Quite clearly, as a general rule, one must applaud select committees as an exercise in more open government. And it goes without saying that the Public Accounts Committee must do its job. But whether this makes named, individual civil servants publicly responsible for their actions is a different matter. Joel Barnett thinks a caning from the Public Accounts Committee can have permanent effects.

> *Barnett*:
> I know from my own experience in the past that this is the occasion, once or twice or three times a year, when the Permanent Secretary, the senior civil servant in the department, is open to public criticism of his management. He prepares himself to the hilt for it, as only a very bright civil servant can, and there is no doubt he takes it very, very seriously indeed. There have been some leading civil servants in the fairly recent past who have been criticised by the Public Accounts Committee,[1] and it clearly has had very serious consequences for them in their careers.

Civil servants, on the other hand, go into some remarkable intellectual contortions to make it clear that before a select committee it's not really they who are being examined – but someone who isn't even in the room. To Tim Nodder, one sentence is enough to describe the true position.

---

1 For example, it was revealed in the course of cross-examination by the PAC on 31 October 1979 that Sir Jack Rampton (Department of Energy) had miscalculated government grants to oil companies by £41 million (HC286). He was correcting a previous admission to the PAC of a miscalculation of £52 million.

Nodder:

I think I would briefly say that the job one has in appearing before a select committee is assisting the minister to be accountable to Parliament.

This seemed a bit too brief and, under massive pressure, Mr Nodder did elaborate. As he sees it, it's only the voice that's the civil servant's.

Nodder:

The minister is accountable to the House and he's accountable in numerous ways – answering parliamentary questions, replying to correspondence from MPs, and taking part in debates. We're concerned in our day-to-day business to assist him with all of these. I see the select committee procedure as an extension of that accountability, and therefore one in which the civil servant is assisting the minister in that process, which in this case involves assisting him to explain and justify himself and his policies to a select committee.

Nor was Mr Nodder being in any way eccentric in this claim to a position which is, it seems, at every stage tied to that of his minister. His boss, Patrick Nairne, also refuses to see the civil servant as being accountable directly to Parliament or, hence, to the public.

Nairne:

I think what it has meant, and I think it's a good thing, is that civil servants themselves have had to expound on policies and have had to be capable of explaining the reasons behind these policies to committees. The important point of principle is that civil servants, in doing that, have remained accountable to their ministers. They haven't become accountable to the committees themselves, but they have in a sense become answerable to the committees for that part of policy-making that falls to civil servants.

Even this limited role, however, has its *longueurs*. Sir Ian Bancroft just said he was in favour of the select committee system, now expanded from the days of Samuel Pepys. But he is honest enough to admit that these committees can be a big nuisance. Civil servants, you see, live their entire lives under Parliament's inconvenient impositions, and select committees are no exception.

Bancroft:

They're a diversion of effort, of course, but so are adjournment debates, so are parliamentary questions, and I think that it's bred in the bones of civil servants over many years, that supporting ministers in accountability to Parliament is one of the most vital things that they have to do. So I think that anyone who regarded them in general as a nuisance would not be thinking very sensibly, though there are occasions when, on a particular issue or on a particular line of inquiry, one might find them just a touch irritating or perhaps faintly wasteful of time.

To go back to the question we began with: if, as is entirely credible, the parliamentary mechanisms are sometimes an irritating waste of time, when *do* civil servants recognise a direct, personal duty to account for themselves to the voters? It may surprise you to know that there are some areas where they do. Take, at a rather low level, the Child Benefit office headquarters in Newcastle-upon-Tyne. The Newcastle Central Office as a whole, covering many other welfare payments as well, deals with 60,000 queries a day. Among the many things they pride themselves on up there is their availability to the public at large. John Milne is the Senior Principal in charge of Child Benefits.

Milne:

It's quite understandable for people to think that we are faceless bureaucrats but we are now moving over to more accountable management, more involvement with the public. My people are encouraged to write to individuals, to telephone individuals, and I think we're gradually getting over to the public at large that we're not faceless bureaucrats. In addition, they have the local office network and they can go and see people in the local offices and talk to people about their Child Benefit problems. These problems, if they can't be resolved locally, are passed up here and we, again in a human sort of way, try to resolve them, by correspondence if possible, but if necessary we do ring people up.

Indeed, when British Rail were offering rock-bottom excursion fares to old-age pensioners, an alarming number of them used them to take day-trips to Newcastle, to make personal representations about their pensions. And Sir Patrick Nairne agrees that individual case-work is an area where civil servants should be made accountable. He also admits that, in spite of these efforts, things can go wrong.

Nairne:

Now this does naturally worry me. Sometimes they go wrong, I think, because civil servants are perhaps insensitive to what the impact of government can be on individuals. Sometimes they go wrong because the civil service can be extraordinarily slow, disgracefully slow occasionally, in dealing with letters and correspondence, often correspondence about very difficult and complicated matters. The more urgent political business that they're dealing with tends to take priority. The only protection against this is, first, that people should be ready – as most people are, I think – to complain very quickly to their Members of Parliament, to get on to the minister, to write to the top of the department. If the worst comes to the worst, they can complain to the Ombudsman. That, if you like, is the side where the consumer can do something about it. On our side, I think it's a question of good training and we certainly try in our training to educate all civil servants about their very real responsibilities.

Even here, however, the long arm of the civil service reaches out to grab the luckless minister by the neck. Of course, not all civil servants would put it that way, but Ian Bancroft, as head of the service, is surely an authority – and he testifies that even the humblest official is in some crucial sense acting on behalf of his minister.

Bancroft:

Now that doesn't mean to say that the counter clerk at a local office in a particular region who takes a decision is involving the minister with it. He's not. Or she's not. That decision is taken by the particular clerk *but*, although he's got responsibility for it, he has not got the entire responsibility. The minister also has got a responsibility. And for why? Because the individual official has had no say in the policy that he's administering and no say in the resources that he's been given. Now he may regard the policy as barmy; he may regard the resources as too few. In that event what he's got to do is to report his views up the line. If his views are accepted, fine. If they're not, then he's got two courses: he can resign or he can get on with the job. In that way there's this rather subtle relationship, at whatever level.

Nor is that the end of the minister's part by a long way. When he's laid down his policy, it seems, he must simply take on trust that it will be properly executed. If in the execution it does go wrong, he should know where his obligations lie.

Bancroft:

The minister can't pretend to know all that's being done in his name. What he's got to do is to lay down the policy and how he wants the policy carried out, and then trust the officials to carry it out efficiently, economically and effectively. And it's the job of the officials if need be, after discussing with the minister, to carry that out faithfully and loyally, whether or not they agree with it. Similarly, if you have a particular policy which leads to crowds of angry customers round the counter or disappointed companies who haven't got their grants, because of the minister's policy, then I think the officials are entitled to look to the minister for loyalty and support. So it's a rather subtle two-way stretch.

But that answer surely begs a question about the policy itself, and who should take any responsibility for it. It's a question to which civil servants have a studiously simple and disarming answer. To outsiders it is at least a fair notion to suggest that, whatever the textbooks say, civil servants cannot totally disclaim responsibility or excuse themselves of all blame for particular advice they give. At the very least, we suggested to several of them, some part of the blame for the last twenty years of British history – years, we could surely agree, of relative failure – should be attached to the continuing government in Whitehall, as well as to Cabinets that have come and gone. Let's hear first what a veteran politician, Lord Soames, thinks about this revolutionary idea.

Soames:

I think we all carry our responsibilities. I think every citizen carries his responsibilities for this, and to that extent the civil service must, too; they've given advice, be it good or be it bad, be it indifferent, but ministers have to take the responsibility. They are dependent, of course they are, on advice which they get from the civil servants, and the senior civil servants carry a heavy responsibility in this regard. But a good minister is there in order to be able to make up his own mind and can't go squealing afterwards, 'Well, I was advised of this by the civil service. It's their fault.'

> Then the answer is, 'Well, if he was wrong, he ought to have been put out.'

But it is perhaps the decisive difference between a minister and an official that the latter, according to Ian Bancroft, is not to be held systematically to account for the quality of the advice he gives.

> *Bancroft*:
> If the advice was, as I assume it must have been, honestly given on the facts available and accepted by the ministers of the day, I don't think I myself would want to see a large label hung around that man's neck for the rest of his career, saying he gave the wrong advice on a particular subject. It will be apparent to his peers that he had given the wrong advice, and the grapevine in the civil service, as in any other large organisation, is a fairly powerful one.

But the test of wrongness, even if it is attempted, can often be made only years after the advice was given – a point which even Lord Soames, not by any means an enemy of the mandarins, finds hard to take.

> *Soames*:
> You don't get punished, inasmuch as your career doesn't come to an end, if you give a bad bit of advice. But perhaps you're listened to less. The trouble is, very often it isn't found out for a long time afterwards. I mean, if it's advice about something that's going to happen tomorrow, it's easier to see. You can measure it, as it were. But if you take the role of the Treasury, for instance, in the economic and financial decisions that have been made over the last twenty or thirty years, you can ask, 'Why is it that our productivity is so much lower in this country and our production has increased so much less than it has in many of our competitor countries in recent years?' You can't blame that just on governments, though governments have undoubtedly played their part in it; you can't say that the civil service, in the advice they've given, have had nothing to do with it at all.

To which top civil servants make roughly two kinds of reply. One is foreshadowed by what Lord Soames went on to say.

> *Soames*:
> It's part of the nation; it's part of our country; it's part of our malaise; it's part of the troubles that we're going through.

Or, in that famous cop-out which dispels blame by spreading it so thin that it disappears, 'We are all guilty'. Ian Bancroft admits partial responsibility, but is happier to emphasise its collective aspect.

Bancroft:

We're all in the dock together. And the more that one tries to say, 'Well, it's section A or section B or section C of the community that's to blame', I think the less chance there is of getting out of the mess we're in.

The other response is to deny, or at least greatly diminish, the scale of this mess: no mess, therefore no blame. That's what Michael Partridge, another Deputy Secretary at DHSS, after a modest disclaimer, seemed to be saying when asked whether the civil service was in any way responsible for Britain's failure.

Partridge:

I think that's a very difficult one. It's really probably for people outside the civil service to answer that. I think we British tend to denigrate ourselves a lot. In fact, we have achieved a lot and particularly in the area I've been interested in, social security, I think we have achieved a great deal over the last twenty years. We've had a complete revision of every aspect of social security and the credit for that belongs to ministers, but also I think to civil servants. There are obviously areas in which we haven't been so successful, and I suppose it's true there that everybody concerned takes some blame, but I don't think it's really just ministers and the civil service. The sort of services you get are the sort of services that people are prepared to pay for; ministers, after all, have to get the legislation through Parliament. The blame is shared really throughout the nation.

By the end of that, as you'll have noticed, Mr Partridge was slipping into the 'we are all guilty' camp. No such back-sliding by Patrick Nairne.

Nairne:

Well, I don't quite know why you're talking about blame. I had a short period of working on the European Community and for the last five to six years I've been in the DHSS. Most of my life, though, has been spent working in the area of defence. I was only one of a very large team there, but I think that the defence policies that this country, as part of a major treaty organisation, has followed, what-

> ever government has been in power, have been remarkably successful. And I think that civil servants are entitled to take some credit for that, as well as ministers.

But surely, by extension, that must mean taking blame as well for other things, like the economy, which have not been quite so successful. Was this a reluctant admission at last? If so, it was plainly an inadvertent one. Of the four questions we've asked about the civil service in these programmes so far – is it too powerful? too big? incompetent? unaccountable? – this is the one which has been answered most clearly by the civil servants themselves. Mainly they are not, and feel they should not be, accountable to anyone except their minister. A situation, combined with their power, which is ripe for fundamental re-examination and which we'll discuss again at the end of the series.

Brussels: A Mandarin's Paradise?

First broadcast: 12 July 1981

The hidden arm of Whitehall lies across the Channel, in Brussels. It is 'hidden' not because of any great secret about British membership of the European Community but because hardly anyone understands how deeply this fact has imposed itself on the way our governing classes spend their time. For some departments, like the Foreign Office and the Ministry of Agriculture, it is *the* dominating premise of their professional lives. In others – Energy, Industry, Trade – it gives work to a lot of officials who wouldn't otherwise have been needed. High-class officials, too, by their account. Some of them work in Brussels at the United Kingdom delegation there. Unusually, people are seconded to this particular embassy from all over Whitehall, but they are always, according to Brian Crowe, the Foreign Office's number two man there, the *crème de la crème.*

> *Crowe*:
> One of the requirements of a posting here is that people should be of the highest quality and the Permanent Representative does have the right, which he does very occasionally exercise, of turning people down because he does not think they're suitable for some reason. So we can ensure that we get only the very best people here.

Not merely the quality but the sheer numbers involved also indicate Whitehall's priorities. First there is the permanent delegation, but next the positive army of officials who keep the airlines in business. Many of them come from the Ministry of Agriculture, where the Permanent Secretary is Sir Brian Hayes.

> *Hayes*:
> On average, 200 of my staff go to Brussels every month to attend meetings that the Commission or the Council calls. But very many more are affected one way or another by decisions of the Council of Ministers and of the Commission in Brussels. Agricultural policy is the only true common policy in the Community, and agricultural policy in the United Kingdom therefore forms a part of the Common Agricultural Policy.

A development which, according to Peter Walker, the Minister of Agriculture, has transformed his ministry, not merely into an outward-looking department, but one populated by men of tigerish calibre.

Walker:

It is quite a tribute to the civil service that a department which was, I suppose, the most inward-looking and domestically-oriented department in Whitehall until we joined the Community,[1] now probably has the best negotiating team (I'm talking about officials, no flattery to the ministers) in Brussels of any member country.

Look at this account of civil service excellence and ministerial contentment through the prism of anti-Market sentiment, however, and you come up with a different picture. The very fact that it is the best people who are sent to work in Brussels, that scores of them travel there to meet and negotiate, and that they become so damned good at it, can make some ministers feel forlorn and out of control, impotent before the combined prejudices of their own departmental officials, the Foreign Office and that great pullulating organism of bureaucrats which runs the Common Market, the European Commission. In his days as a minister at the Departments of Energy and Industry, Tony Benn[2] used to present this picture of himself with abject candour – and the memory of it has not faded.

Benn:

There were one or two officials in Brussels all the time, and I had some links with them, who would go in for package deals. They would then come and tell you about a package deal when it was too late to unpick it. That was one problem. The other problem was, of course, that the Foreign Office, for example, would insist on putting the Commission first. I remember one flaming row with the Foreign Office when they said that I couldn't even publish the Industry Bill in 1975 until the Commission had approved the Bill in draft, before it was published by the House of Commons. I absolutely declined to agree and the Bill was published. But I've no doubt that that Bill had been shown to the Commission before it was shown to the House of Commons.

---

1 On 1 January 1973.

2 Tony Benn was Secretary of State for Industry 1974–5 and for Energy 1975–9.

This is sufficient proof in Mr Benn's mind of the truth of a phrase he once used in a different place to sum up Brussels. He called it a 'mandarin's paradise'. And, visiting the place, one can see what he meant. To help you get around, they give you not a map but an aerial photograph, in the middle of which stands the Berlaymont building, where the Commission is housed, a veritable temple of mandarin worship. Pompous, many-faced and built to conform with a finely-graded hierarchy of status, this structure is a more exact emblem of what goes on inside it than any other public building we've come across. Radiating out, its four wings look like tentacles, ready to ensnare all the buildings within its reach. On one corner, the UK Representative's office with heavily armed policemen on guard outside, on another the Charlemagne building where most of the meetings we attended took place. Here flourish working groups, working parties, committees, special committees, subcommittees and councils in all the bewildering variety which makes them so beloved of the officials who know how to manipulate them. Committees, however, do mean work. If they are revelling in some kind of Utopia of power, Whitehall's transient exiles have to pay a price. Peter Pooley is the senior Ministry of Agriculture man in the UK delegation and describes a life that takes at least some of the shine off paradise.

Pooley:

The week starts on a Sunday when, between taking my small boy to his football match and having lunch, I come into the office to pick up my briefs that have arrived from Whitehall for the meeting on Monday and Tuesday, either of the special committee, the official-level body, which is three weeks a month, or of the Council where I'll be assisting the minister. I have to get those briefs swotted up – there can be something like twenty items and the briefs can be two or three inches thick – collate them with the papers that come from the Council's secretariat and be fully briefed and ready to negotiate before I go to bed on Sunday night.

Then there may be one of those famous all-night meetings the Community is so fond of.

Pooley:

Monday and Tuesday we have our meetings. These can go on for a great while: typically at official level from nine o'clock in the morning till eight or nine o'clock at night; at ministerial level a great deal longer and one can have a

> night out of bed or sometimes two on the trot. Wednesday we do our reporting to Whitehall and others who are interested. Other people often are, like the New Zealand mission here on New Zealand butter and lamb that we've talked about a good deal. Or the trade interests.

And then a weekly trip back to Whitehall to sort out instructions for the next gruelling week.

Pooley:

> Thursday I go to London and there I go to the Ministry of Agriculture to take part in the meeting of officials which winds up what happened on the previous Monday and Tuesday. They already have their written reports but face-to-face conversation is so much more helpful. It also decides what form of briefing we need for the next Monday or Tuesday Council or special committee; what lines need to be cleared with other departments and with the minister before we put pen to paper on the instructions; and how we shall handle things tactically.

Visiting Brussels a little while ago, we saw how little these constant to-ings and fro-ings accord with anyone's idea of paradise. One committee was meeting to fix the tender price of sugar, but the British representative had got herself caught up in an air-traffic controllers' strike, so she wasn't there. Another committee was meeting to discuss, for the umpteenth time, the pros and cons of hormone implants in farm animals. The face of the particular official engaged on that one – his air journey made the night before, the prospect quite uncertain of his item even being reached on that day's agenda – did not betray much halcyon delight. What Peter Pooley just said, however, gets near to the real issue, which is not so much how pleasurable or otherwise the life of a Brussels-oriented civil servant is, but how independently powerful it makes him. Is it a place where, because of distance and because there are so many decisions to be taken, the lines of distinction between decisions taken properly by politicians and those taken improperly by officials have become blurred? Sir Donald Maitland is now Permanent Secretary at the Department of Energy but, quite unusually, went there after a career in the Foreign Office, latterly as Britain's Permanent Representative to the European Communities.

Maitland:

> I'm not sure whether mandarins ever actually aspire to paradise, but I don't really recognise the kind of life that I

> led in Brussels when I hear that description. To the outside observer, some distance away from the process of taking decisions in Brussels, it may seem that this dividing line is blurred. But I can only say with the greatest emphasis that for those who actually take part in that process there is no blurring of the line. The line is absolutely clear. Even if, say, the Committee of Permanent Representatives is dealing with a particularly detailed and complex problem, each one of those Representatives (there are now ten round the table) will be acting in accordance with instructions from his government, and those instructions will have been endorsed by a minister.

Even more thoroughly is this imprinted on the minds of junior civil servants. Sandra Brown is a Principal in the division of Sir Donald's department which deals with British energy interests in the Community. From appliance labelling and the sale of coke to energy conservation and price fixing, these are immense. Officials inhabit layer upon layer of committees but always yoked, she says, to their political master.

> *Brown*:
> There are a number of layers of committees even at official level. A question would first of all move between the official committee at my level and the senior official committee, which would act as a co-ordination between what ministers wanted and the ministerial directives to officials and the ordinary level committee doing the work day by day and week by week. There would be a constant interchange between these committees so that official-level committees were, if you like, kept on the broad course that ministers wanted, and so that any problems which arose at official level could fairly readily and smoothly be lifted to senior official level or to ministerial level for resolution.

In Brussels itself self-abnegation also appears to be the name of the game. The Environment Department's man there is Giles Paxman.

> *Paxman*:
> Obviously in the course of a meeting one is called upon to take the decision as to the strength and determination with which one should pursue a particular line of attack, given the opposition that appears to be coming from different quarters. But as regards Yes or No decisions, then I would say that there is, in the normal course of negotiations, a

> let-out that always enables one in cases of doubt to refer back to London.

This let-out is equally useful to the top man in the delegation. According to Donald Maitland, the constant link with home base is part and parcel of everyday life.

> *Maitland*:
> I myself used to find in Brussels that there were times in a debate when my instructions left me in an untenable position. In which case I would ask for a period to reflect on this and I would ask the chairman, 'Could we come back to this item later in the day?' A lot of telephoning between Brussels and London would then take place, and I would hope to receive a message later in the day saying, 'The minister agrees to amend your instructions in the following respect.' And when we got back to this item, the chairman would say, 'I wonder if you have completed your reflection by telephone?', as it is called euphemistically there, and then we would be able to proceed. Now I was in that position from time to time, but so were all my colleagues and there is, as you may know, a considerable machinery at the London end for ensuring the co-ordination of instructions to our representatives in Brussels and ensuring that there is political cover, political authority, for the line which we are going to take.

The relationship, however, is not simply a defensive one, making sure of political cover and so on. It can be a good deal more than that: a creative combination of specifically different powers. Peter Pooley, our man on the special agricultural committee, noticed this when the British were seeking concessions for New Zealand lamb and butter.

> *Pooley*:
> What really gained the day for us was recalling the Community to its sense of political commitment, which is very much easier for a minister to do than for an official. And one can contrast that with a recent deal which was concluded at exactly the same time in the same package, on the Commission's policy towards subsidies on farm structure, which was very technical and detailed. The elements of the bargain were set up between officials – my colleagues and I in the special committee. They had to be done that way because they were issues of the sort that did not involve a major political dimension, and had we left that

> issue to ministers, they would have really had a struggle to arrive at agreement on it. As it was, the special committee spent four or five hundred hours, I should think, arguing over these issues. Ministers spent four or five hours, and it was settled. So there we prepared the ground and I did a job that Peter Walker could not have done. Equally, on New Zealand lamb and mutton, a great deal more political an issue, he did a job that it was absolutely inconceivable that I or any other official could have done.

Peter Walker was in Brussels at the same time as we were and he kindly spirited us into the fringes of the agriculture council meeting he was attending, the preliminaries of which you occasionally catch a glimpse of on the television news. Officials had done a lot of groundwork for the meeting. But the moment Mr Walker stepped into the room, you knew he was a politician. As he circled the table, greeting each minister from the other countries, what he was really doing was nosing out their negotiating position, and quite quickly wheeling and dealing for advantage himself before the meeting so laboriously prepared for by his officials had even begun.

All in all, it seems the evidence we've heard is right: Brussels is not a mandarin's playground in the sense of letting civil servants off the leash of the constitution and giving them enormous untrammelled power. On the contrary, the opposite is truer: that in this area of government activity, as in few others, the lines of political control are drawn tight.

But that's not the end of the story. Even if Britain's entry into the Common Market has not increased mandarin power specifically, it has certainly reorganised the balance of power inside Whitehall itself. The Foreign Office has become a spectacular new power centre on domestic questions. It negotiated British entry and it supervises present relations. And if you were Tony Benn, you would say it has also done something else.

> *Benn*:
> I think the Foreign Office in a deep way has transferred its allegiance from Britain to Brussels. I don't know how long it took to do, because I wasn't a minister during the crucial years from 1970 to 1974, but the European integration department of the Foreign Office (and this came out in a book[1]

1 Geoffrey Moorhouse, *The Diplomats: The Foreign Office Today*, Cape, 1977.

> called *The Diplomats* by Geoffrey Moorhouse) did at that time undoubtedly transfer their allegiance. I had much more difficulty with the Foreign Office than I did with the Commission, in fairness, although the Commission were very difficult and they thought they had the law behind them, the Treaty of Rome. I think the Foreign Office influence on Whitehall is now quite pernicious because the Foreign Office can properly claim that every bit of economic policy, industrial policy, social policy, is now European policy and has to be fed through them. If they think it will interfere with our relations with our partners in the Community they will veto it, if they can, in Whitehall. If it isn't vetoed in Whitehall, they will be party to the process by which the Brussels Commission might veto it. And that is a fundamental change in allegiance.

To which the Foreign Office itself replies with uncomprehending disdain. Our present ambassador to the European Communities is Sir Michael Butler.

Butler:

> I think that's a rather odd statement. I was responsible, in a large measure, for doing the renegotiation of the terms of entry for Mr Callaghan in 1974/5 and I don't think that any of my colleagues in the Community would have been heard commenting that I'd sold my soul to the Community. I think they thought that I was representing the British government's interests and carrying out its instructions. The same would certainly be true of the very arduous negotiations which we had here after the meeting in Strasbourg of the European Council in June 1979 at which Mrs Thatcher got some movement going towards the settlement of the budget, which culminated on 30 May 1980 in us getting back very, very large sums of money, both for the 1980 budget and the 1981 budget and a firm assurance for 1982. I think that you would have been hard-pressed to find any of my colleagues in the Committee of Permanent Representatives who thought that I was selling out to the Community rather than carrying out instructions of the British government and pursuing British interests.

Tony Benn, however, isn't alone in seeing the Foreign Office's true position as slightly more complex than that. He, of course, is an anti-Marketeer. Roy Hattersley is strongly pro-Market but still has few illusions about the Foreign Office's appetite for power – or about any minister's for that matter. It all depends where you're sitting.

Hattersley:

> The Foreign Office holds two views about Europe: one is on the national interest of being in, the second is on what Europe does for the Foreign Office. The Foreign Office has been transformed by our membership of the EEC. It now interferes in and is concerned with subjects which were not its proper province ten years ago. Foreign Office civil servants are interfering in agricultural prices; they're interfering in economic policy; they're interfering in energy policy. Naturally enough, the Foreign Office has an enthusiasm for continuing an institution that gives them this very substantial increased power, and I suspect that ministers whom they point that out to become enthusiastic as well. Even Mr Benn, I think, if he was Foreign Secretary, would like the idea of being able to interfere in everybody else's ministry thanks to the EEC. The great Harvard dictum of government is, 'Where you stand depends on where you sit', and if I were Secretary of State for Energy, I'm sure I'd be deeply irked by the fact that every time I wanted to take a decision about coal or gas prices, somebody from the Foreign Office would be saying, 'Is that consistent with our European obligations? Don't forget my minister, the Foreign Secretary, may have to discuss it at the Council of Ministers in Brussels.' But on the other hand, if I were Foreign Secretary, being human, I think I would like the idea that there was an overall view of these matters and that *I* as Foreign Secretary had a relationship with them that I didn't have before we entered the EEC.

So, what do we have here? A community in which officials seem to exhibit an almost pathological anxiety to get political clearance for every last penny they're committing the country to. But also one where the main custodian of the British interest is the Foreign Office, which has become, to some of the domestic departments, almost upsettingly powerful in the scheme of things. Worst of all, according to an anti-Market minister like Tony Benn, it is the repository of power and influence quite exceeding anything a lone politician can hope to bring to bear.

But there's something else as well. Added to this institutional bias is the fact that Community business is all about negotiation – and negotiation with a view to success, not failure.

Which, as Michael Butler says, involves give and take, which in turn, if you're the giving department, may seem irksome.

> *Butler*:
>
> Our task is to ensure that British interests are protected, while of course always paying reasonable attention to the interests of other member states. Quite often, for example, it's a good idea for us to go out of our way to ensure that important interests of some other member state are met, provided that they don't clash with our own.

In the special agricultural committee, likewise, there's a desire, which home-grown politicians would not all appreciate, for the group to succeed as well as the individual country – although Peter Pooley says, reassuringly, that this falls well short of the great dream of Europe and all that stuff.

> *Pooley*:
>
> You are pulled in these two directions. First, all of us want to do the very best we can for our governments and negotiate as hard as we can. You want to succeed personally and in the special committee, or any other body; you want your point of view to prevail, you want to be seen to win. But you want the committee to win as well, in that you want the committee to reach agreement, put up the dossier, the file, in good form for ministers to negotiate upon. You want to clear as much of the unimportant muck out of the way as you can. You want to belong to a successful group of people that you can be proud to belong to. This happens in any group. This is not a great deal to do with wanting to build Europe. We don't think in such large philosophical terms while we're in committee. It's only after dinner and after the second bottle that one tends to go into such rhapsodies. But we do think a good deal about the special committee putting up a good show. We are strongly linked together by the fact that we see so much of one another and we want other people, the group, to succeed as well as ourselves as individuals.

Behind the headlines about national splits and disagreements that is very much the real spirit of Brussels. And it all feels a long way from Britain and British politics in one important particular. There's absolutely no sense of argument about the principle of the Community's existence or British membership of it. In Britain, as recent opinion polls have shown, half the country might like to get out – more than in any other member state.[1] As Michael Butler says, in one respect this degree of hostility actually increases the degree of political control.

> *Butler*:
>
> It means that I'm particularly closely watched by ministers. Some of my colleagues from other member states have a lot more latitude than I do, because on the whole range of issues their ministers are not deeply concerned about matters that are being discussed here. British ministers are very deeply concerned because they know that everything about the Community is controversial in the UK and they're going to have to debate it in the House of Commons, answer questions in the House of Commons or the House of Lords and so on.

All the same, this raises the bull point both about British policy towards the Market and about our subject, which is how flexible Whitehall really is. One test of this is to ask how responsive it would be to a new political will: or, on the contrary, whether it is so deeply committed to British membership that final proof of the true ownership of this part of paradise would become evident, ironically, at the moment when a government was elected which wanted to take Britain out. Would this not, at the very least, produce the greatest mobilisation of mandarin power even Whitehall has ever seen? Or would it simply be accepted as the textbooks say it should be? Sir Donald Maitland, at the Department of Energy, is the most spartan of textbook-men.

> *Maitland*:
>
> I don't think that there would be any problems of the kind that you describe. I think your second alternative is correct. This would be a political decision which the departments concerned would carry out to the best of their ability.

And even at the Ministry of Agriculture, says Sir Brian Hayes, a British exit is not unthinkable.

> *Hayes*:
>
> Oh, I think it's thinkable. It could be that one day we would have a government which decided to take us out and in that case the civil servants would have to carry out that policy. But it is true that we accept it perhaps to a greater degree than some elements of the public do, simply because we have to work within the system. The system is now part of the life of Whitehall, particularly part of the life of

1 For example, a MORI poll published in March 1981 found that 64% wanted Britain to withdraw from the EEC and only 36% wanted to stay in.

this department. The Ministry of Agriculture can't help but be conscious of UK membership of the Community because, as you know, about three-quarters of the Community budget is agricultural and about ninety per cent of Community legislation is agricultural. But were there ever to be a change of policy, that too would have to be carried out.

Peter Walker, his minister, is equally sanguine about the due processes of the law transcending any notion that it would somehow be impossible to get out.

Walker:

I don't think that is so. There are times at about three o'clock in the morning when the whole of this department would happily leave the EEC. And you know, if a future government made a decision to withdraw from the EEC, a department like this would very quickly get to work on whatever national agricultural policy would take its place. The speed with which the department moved from being a domestic department to a European one was very impressive, and if political decisions, or whatever else in history, decide in the future that it should change, I think the change would take place.

But in Brussels there's a lot more soul-searching. Speaking as a negotiator, Peter Pooley reckons it might give him employment but would deal him an atrocious hand to play.

Pooley:

Well, you're touching on major politics here, so I draw down the asbestos shield on what my thoughts are for a moment or two. Just speaking entirely frivolously, one is encouraged by the thought that all experience shows that it takes a great many more civil servants to run something down than to run it up, so the career prospects in the short term might be not unattractive. But the thought of withdrawal and negotiating the withdrawal is rather appalling to us in a way. If we're told to do it, of course we'll do it. But it is a major task given that if we decide to move out there won't be anybody here who will owe us any favours or will want to make the way easy for us. Rather the reverse. We will be mucking up things for them good and proper and they will feel no obligation, so far as I can see, to ease our way, give us special concessions, make sure that the penalties of withdrawal, which are considerable, are ameliorated because we're nice chaps and they don't want us to fail. They will regard us as being not very nice chaps and they couldn't care less whether we fail or succeed.

From the Foreign Office, on the other hand, Michael Butler thinks he might have to resign. But then again he might not. Either way, here speaks a civil servant not afraid to admit to a deeply-held conviction.

Butler:

Well, you're asking me there to embark on ground which maybe goes a little bit beyond where we should go in this interview. I mean, of course, the duty of any civil servant is to carry out the instructions of his ministers, but he also in the end has the option of resigning if the policy which the ministers of the day adopt is not one that he feels, in all conscience, he can follow. Certainly I might find myself in such a position, because I think that the interests of this country are profoundly bound up with membership of the Community and I think that it would, in fact, be impossible to leave the Community without leaving the Western industrialised world. I think that our membership of the Community is now so much a part of the national life that it would be very difficult for any government to take us out of the Community. I think really that would have to be something that, if I was still in this job at the time, I would have to consider. I certainly carried out the instructions of the Labour government when they came to power in 1974, without any difficulty to my conscience. I thought our approach was very fully in accordance with the national interest and I pursued their instructions with zeal, and it may be that I would be able to do the same another time.

Some people would be horrified if many civil servants became as closely involved as that with what is far from being a bipartisan policy. Does it not infringe the Whitehall rule that civil servants should not have strong opinions? Earlier, we heard from a senior mandarin that this was the very definition of unacceptable eccentricity. Whether or not most officials conform to this rule, one does not know. But what is axiomatic to the British way of governing is that they should at least pretend not to have these opinions, the better to serve any political master the electorate throws up. Next – and finally – we examine the merit of that axiom: whether Britain wouldn't be better off with civil servants who really did believe what their minister believed; who didn't say No, but Yes, minister – and meant it.

Who are the Masters Now?

First broadcast: 19 July 1981

We've asked five questions in this series and resisted the temptation to offer glib answers to any of them. Is the civil service too big? Probably, but they're working on it. Is it incompetent? Probably not, but the kind of competence most admired in civil servants is open to question. Is it unaccountable in the sense that most people understand the word? Yes – but in that sense they don't even want to be. And what about Brussels? Is that the peak of civil service freedom from political control? The answer here was clearer: an almost emphatic negative. The fifth question was, in order, the first we asked: is the civil service too powerful? It's also the one to which the answer is most opaque, yet the one at the heart of everything. Who are the masters now – in this age when government, like life, is so enormously complex, when a thousand decisions a day may be made in the name of ministers and when the fear of absolute national decline becomes an ever more urgent imperative? And if it's the mandarins who are the masters (always favouring continuity over change) can anything be done to reassert the position of the democratically elected politician? As we shall hear, today's Tories and yesterday's Socialists are deeply ambivalent about this question. It is, however, rendered a good deal more acute by the change that's come over politics in the last ten years, the lurch of both main parties to the extremes. Shirley Williams, an apostle of the centre, is in a good position to identify the consequences.

Williams:

It's not just the civil servants, it's the counterpoint, the fugue between civil servants and politicians, that in my view has had a lot to do with the decline of this country. On the one side you have the civil servants, as you rightly say, genuinely preaching continuity and consensus and generally eschewing radical ideas whether of the right or the left. And then you have the politicians exercising their muscles and increasingly trying to establish a kind of machismo image by beating the civil servants over the head and moving more and more to the extremes precisely to show who's boss. So you've really got the worst of both worlds.

> You've got a kind of deeply incompatible marriage going on here.

For their part of this marriage the civil servants, as Shirley Williams said, have a bias in favour of the conservative virtues of caution, continuity and the like. But this is a bit more than a purely self-interested belief in creating an easy life for themselves. They see themselves, Environment minister Michael Heseltine says, as having continuing responsibilities as custodians of something higher than the passing fad of a new political idea. That something is the quality of public administration.

> *Heseltine*:
>
> They are cautious people because the degree of criticism for failure is enormous and the credit for success a great deal less in public administration. They've been brought up in a tradition where they've seen every new idea explored and many of them rejected; it isn't often that you present them with something that's not been put in front of them before. And they feel a great loyalty to their own service and to the politicians who serve them, not to let that politician get himself into a ludicrous situation.

Although that's a politician speaking, it puts the civil service view very clearly. But the view from the other side of this incompatible liaison is put with equally exquisite diplomacy by Tony Benn. As politicians, there are similarities between Mr Benn and Mr Heseltine. Both are self-preoccupied, extraordinarily sure of themselves, with more friends outside Parliament than in. But Mr Benn sees civil servants quite differently: as wielders of calculated and negative power.

> *Benn*:
>
> They are always trying to steer incoming governments back to the policy of the outgoing government, minus the mistakes that the civil service thought the outgoing government made. And remember, when a government is elected it has maximum energy and minimum knowledge. Just before it's defeated it has maximum knowledge and minimum energy, and the civil service can deploy their influence to beat an outgoing government into the acceptance of an easy course. They then have to slow down an incoming government from the course they think to be advisable. That is the meaning, really, of the civil service being the architects of, and advocates of, and continuing administrators of consensus politics.

Although this problem is given greater sharpness in an age when the politics of the parties is dominated by rejection of consensus, it's not in fact a new one. As long ago as 1964 a new Whitehall species was born: the political or special adviser, half-politician and half-official, was designed to make the uneasy marriage a smoother relationship. Some people have attached great importance to this innovation, welcoming it almost ecstatically as the key to the mystery of government – namely, how an apolitical civil service can truly serve a very political minister. Bernard Donoughue was special adviser at 10 Downing Street to both Harold Wilson and Jim Callaghan.

Donoughue:

In my view it's the most important development in modern government in Britain. The machine is now so powerful and the career civil service so big and so influential, and with the capacity effectively to control many ministers, that ministers need an alternative source of advice and information. They need an alternative source that's operating within the machine so that they have access to all the resources of the machine and so they can argue with the civil service and come to understand what they are going for. They need to have an alternative voice and, of course, to have a political dimension. The fact is that ministers, the political executive, are political, they do have a party base, they do have a constituency in the country. They do have political commitments, they do have a political philosophy. There's no need to be ashamed of that. I think it's quite silly the way people pretend, and often the civil service pretends, that this political dimension is somehow something to be ashamed of and something to be got round.

And there's no doubt that a minister coming fresh to his department can be both aided and comforted by the presence close to him of a really reliable sympathiser. From Roy Hattersley's memory of the Department of Prices and Consumer Protection, one gets a picture of the sheer ego-boosting a minister needs, which civil servants would recoil from offering but with which he was supplied by a very special adviser.

Hattersley:

He was Professor Maurice Peston[1] who, from my point of

1 Maurice Peston, Professor of Economics at Queen Mary College, London, was special adviser to the Department of Education 1974–5, and to the Department of Prices and Consumer Protection 1976–9.

> view, had the supreme advantage of sharing almost exactly my political beliefs. We both believed that we occupied the same position in the socialist spectrum: the Tawney/Cole/Crosland position. We both believed in the direct intervention of the government in the economy. In his phrase, we thought that the Department of Prices had the primary job of setting the guidelines for the mixed economy: how companies worked, levels of competition, attack on monopolies, control of prices, influence of advertising. We thought that was the department's job, and when I arrived at the department very many of the civil servants didn't think that was the department's job, and my task was to convince them that it was. Now having somebody who shared my views almost exactly but could also support them with a body of academic belief, with a substantial academic reputation, with that marvellous cachet of being called a professor, was a major advantage. I remember a slightly disgruntled civil servant saying to Maurice Peston that his task in the department was to give a spurious intellectual justification to my prejudices. Now that's a very pejorative way of describing what he did, but if you put it quite the other way round, you could say that his job was to demonstrate the fundamental wisdom of my beliefs. That's how I would have described what he did.

Not all politicians feel the need for this kind of service. Michael Heseltine points out that a minister doesn't come in alone anyway. Better the full-blooded politician than a kind of bureaucratic half-caste.

Heseltine:

> I've got a very considerable team of political advisers called ministers, and we meet most days in order to discuss any matters that any of them wants to raise and in order to keep up a political momentum. I hope we are a very coherent team in that sense, and I don't subscribe to that great obstructionism which is attributed to the civil service. If there is delay it's my fault and I try to ensure that it doesn't happen.

Whitehall, of course, saw no need for these politically-motivated invaders. They were an affront to everything the civil service stands for: committed, loyal to a party, prejudiced in favour of the answer Yes not No to what the minister wants, and not trapped in a career structure which always ensures that a civil servant's loyalties are divided between the minister and the mandarins above, who will determine his career prospects long after the minister has disappeared.

At first Whitehall saw this experiment as a threat, and therefore froze it out. But later Whitehall got wiser, and even began to find merit, of a strictly peripheral kind, in special advisers. According to Sir Patrick Nairne, they could even offer something a civil servant could not.

Nairne:

It was a kind of extra edge, a sort of extra tang when it came to speech drafting, when it came sometimes to getting just the right thrust to a parliamentary statement in the House, an extra tang that I don't think civil servants can quite provide. I don't think that ministers will ever make a good speech, or at least not a good major speech, unless they dictate a good deal of it themselves. That's what most ministers do. They depend upon briefing notes; they've discussed it with civil servants and civil servants then give them their briefing notes, but in the end they've got to make it their own speech. Now, with the help of a really good political adviser who knows their mind, they can quite often take the political adviser's drafting on the basis of the civil servant's briefing note. I don't think it is something that civil servants do as well as some of those political advisers.

Now, according to Sir Ian Bancroft, the head of the civil service,[1] they are thoroughly approved of: which is perhaps another way of saying that they've been taken on board, absorbed into the system, house-trained, and, as agents of anything like radical change, ever so politely suffocated.

Bancroft:

I've known political advisers or special advisers, whatever you call them, from both parties in a number of departments. For the most part they've been of considerable benefit to the ministers for whom they were working, and in a curious sort of sideways effect also to the departments in which they were working for those ministers, because they do provide an extra dimension in terms of being able to go to meetings, keep up contacts with the party of the day in

1 Until 12 November 1981 when the Civil Service Department was abolished and Sir Ian was prematurely retired. He became a Life Peer in the New Year's Honours List of 1 January 1982.

a way which no civil servant possibly could. It depended very much on the remit that they were given by their minister, the personalities of the minister and the special adviser, and the chemistry that existed between the two of them, and between them and the department. I found them overwhelmingly useful rather than the reverse.

If we're talking about power, power as between ministers and civil servants, that sounds almost like an epitaph on the political-adviser experiment. At best they're a minor cosmetic on the great granite face of the body politic: good for appearances, even for a politician's self-regard, but not likely to change very much. Something along these lines could, of course, do very much more. You could develop a civil service, which, at its most sensitive points, ceased any longer to possess the sacred virtue now attributed to it – its famous impartiality. A more political civil service does exist in Washington and Paris, where new ministers bring with them, or otherwise acquire, a large personal staff of political sympathisers to try and ensure that the potentially incompatible marriage doesn't work out to the politician's disadvantage. In France, and for that matter Brussels and the European Commission, this is known as the minister's *cabinet*. It's not approved in this country, and as Denis Healey reveals, when he informally introduced it for his own particular purposes as Minister of Defence fifteen years ago, it had the kind of consequences which might be a warning to any civil servant who now chose to get too close to a politician.

Healey:

I didn't feel satisfied with all the advice coming to me through the pyramids of the three services, the scientists and the civil service, so I set up a little personal *cabinet* called the Programme Evaluation Group, taking first-rate people in mid-career to make sure I asked the right questions and that when decisions were taken I got relevant answers, and then I got the decisions carried out. I found that immensely valuable, and the people I chose turned out to be very well chosen. One was Neil Cameron[1] who later became the Chief of Defence Staff, although he suffered

1 Marshal of the Royal Air Force Sir Neil Cameron. Programme Evaluation Group, MoD 1965–6; Assistant Chief of Defence Staff (Policy) 1968–70; SASO Air Support Command 1970–2; Deputy Commander RAF, Germany 1972–3; AOC 46 Group Air Staff 1974; Air Member for Personnel, MoD 1974–6; Chief of the Air Staff 1976–7; Chief of the Defence Staff 1977–9.

> very badly in his career through working for me. He was victimised by the Air Force for a couple of years because he'd shown his loyalty to me rather than to his own service.

I think that type of thing could be employed more widely. But it doesn't look as though it will be, at any rate not if Sir Ian Bancroft has anything to do with it. He'd conceded that the special advisers were overwhelmingly useful. So what about a fully-fledged political *cabinet*?

> *Bancroft*:
>
> I ought really to try and dodge that question but I won't. I don't think that would be a good idea in our present system. By all means have special advisers giving a political input but to have the minister of the day walled off from his department by a *cabinet* of people who were specially chosen for their political affiliations would, I think, tend to lead to an alienation between the minister and his department which would not be very sensible or healthy.

For Patrick Nairne any such prospect summons up the image not so much of prison walls as of a malfunctioning internal combustion engine.

> *Nairne*:
>
> I've never been attracted, myself, to a *cabinet* system as an alternative to our system. It is easy to understand that a really good *cabinet* can immediately provide a minister with able people whom he knows are entirely sympathetic to his views, but I don't think they would prove, how shall I say, a good gearbox with the department. They've still got to work to the department.

The gearbox now supplied is one that Whitehall knows very well how to put together; it is the minister's private office. This is the part of the machine where the struggle of wills between politician and civil servant is most obviously acted out. The private office, staffed by the most able young civil servants, is the minister's private retinue. It's there to facilitate his wishes, presumably helping him to get his way inside the department, keeping him in touch with other departments and so on. It's a rare luxury for a politician fresh from opposition to have such service. But it's no use pretending that a private secretary is working solely for his minister. As we've said, it's the service which employs him and has his future in its hands. And he is not left long unaware of the state of mind of his Permanent Secretary, who might, indeed, be Patrick Nairne.

Nairne:

One very common feature of my day is to have a quick few minutes with the principal private secretary. I either walk down the corridor and look in on him and find out what's going on: 'Did all go well in the debate last night?', you know, 'What's emerged from Cabinet this morning?' Or he may look in on me. Or I may come in, very often I do come in, having read something in my overnight papers which I'm not happy about, something that's been put up by one of my colleagues and I want to say to the private secretary, 'Look, don't let the minister take a final decision on this till I've had a word because I'm not altogether happy about what Mr X said.'

Here you can begin to see how the struggle for mastery might work. In a benign department, where minister and officials were at one, this kind of liaison might seem only sensible. But imagine one led by a politician who radically challenged the continuing departmental wisdom. What price then the hot seat between Permanent Secretary and minister? Of course, as Patrick Nairne says, Whitehall is always prepared to change a minister's servants – although perish the thought that this should really be necessary.

Nairne:

It is very easy for a minister to get changes in his private office, if that's what he wants. I think that it would be one of the tests of a good young civil servant that he would be capable of quickly winning the confidence of a new minister when he comes into office. I have certainly had experience in my career of a number of changes having to be made where a new minister coming into office has found somehow that the face hasn't fitted. I think that where that has happened it may not always be the fault of the civil servant, but I do think that it is part of the training of a good civil servant in our service that he should be capable of serving a new master.

And some ministers find that they can exact some sanction against civil servants whose advice they reckon is either not good enough or not what they'd like to hear. Peter Walker, for one.

Walker:

If you're dissatisfied, and I have on some occasions been dissatisfied, then I will go to the Permanent Secretary and I will say to him, 'Look, I think the chap who is advising me on this is not very good, I'm very unimpressed by him. I think the last three minutes he sent me are lousy and this is a very important sphere of my department.' Then the Permanent Secretary will either say he's been ill or something like that or he will have him moved.

That's an important point, but fundamentally it's misleading. It might imply that ministers are often dissatisfied with the civil service or individual civil servants. One overwhelming truth with which one emerges from this journey round Whitehall is that on the whole they very rarely are. Academics, journalists and backbench MPs may castigate the bureaucracy, doubt its competence, question its energy, jealously observe its pretensions to power, but ministers give little hint of this. They tend to marvel at civil servants' industry, integrity and sheer availability. And even if they are critical they don't accept the conventional academic nostrums about what to do about it. Take the most critical of all, Tony Benn. He has no doubt about the nexus between the top civil service and a kind of multi-national onslaught against genuine democracy.

Benn:

Power lies in Britain in certain clear hands. In government it lies in the hands of the Prime Minister and the permanent officials from certain key ministries. Power lies in Brussels now, power lies in America, the Pentagon controls our defence policy, and our intelligence policy is controlled and supervised by the United States. The multi-nationals have great power, the IMF has great power. And if you regard the task of government to come to terms with the inevitable, which is broadly what many senior civil servants would say, what you're saying is democracy could never be strong enough to change the balance of power. Now that's fine for two governments that are much alike in character, one Conservative with the same policy, and one Labour with the same policy, but that is not an adequate explanation or answer for government elected with a commitment to change.

But ask Mr Benn whether a more politicised civil service is the answer and, while insisting that it is too powerful, he doesn't seem to think that changing it is the way out.

Benn:

I'm totally opposed to a spoils system like the one they have in America. That's highly undesirable. I think that the

> civil service by being professional has a great deal to offer. On the other hand their power is too great. I think that when Permanent Secretaries sit down together – they're supposed to call themselves Cabinet 'O', 'O' standing for Official – they do think that they are the ultimate government of the country and that ministers may come and go, but in them resides the ultimate responsibility. I believe they think that, although they recognise that Cabinets may not always uphold their view. So the problem of getting democratic control of the accumulation of power that is vested in the permanent state machine is a formidable one.

No other minister has used that kind of language. On the other hand, while being pretty uncritical of civil servants as a class, ministers who are prepared to look at the service with some detachment home in on one thing Tony Benn was talking about. It's not just socialists or even radicals who see the civil service as observing a kind of remorseless rhythm in support of certain kinds of policy. Men of the centre like Jim Prior, the quintessence of a consensus-minded man, see a two-year cycle in these affairs and are depressed by the consequences.

Prior:

> There is the old adage that it takes two years for ministers to get to know their way about a particular department and then for the last two years they are trying to undo some of the damage that they've done in the first two years. Then the government changes and it takes the civil service another two years to train the new lot. I don't go along with that obviously, but there is a feeling in Whitehall that it is a pretty frustrating business for them having to teach their ministers their jobs. Therefore the whole time you do get the desire of the civil service to keep to the existing policy but to remove the warts from it, and that's a perfectly understandable thing. But that way you wouldn't actually get much thrust in any policy, and you certainly wouldn't get the impact of what one might call, I suppose, democracy or parliamentary government, let alone politics, coming in.

Some people will say that this two-year cycle – and you can find uncanny evidence of it in the history of the last five governments – is a thoroughly good thing. But we're not concerned with that kind of judgement in these programmes. The interesting question is who makes that kind of decision, not whether it's a good one. Top mandarins will go to their graves insisting that it's not them. From any number of disclaimers of power we've collected in Whitehall recently, this one from Sir Donald Maitland will do as well as any.

Maitland:

It is the task of the civil service to advise and support the government in office. So there isn't such a thing as a Department of Energy policy in the energy field. It may appear sometimes that there is something which might look like a departmental policy but that arises from the fact that it is the department's job to put forward the relevant considerations. Now the relevant considerations, in the view of the department, will be the same whether a government is formed from this party or from that party. But in the end the decisions are taken by the ministers and they are carried out by the civil service on behalf of the ministers.

Sir Donald makes the 'relevant considerations' sound as though they're devoid of value-judgements: laundered free of any defacing stain of prejudice. Patrick Nairne, likewise, thinks it's the very detachment of civil servants that makes them so beloved of generations of ministers.

Nairne:

I've worked very closely with senior Cabinet ministers of both parties and, if it doesn't sound egoistic, I think that those particular Cabinet ministers have felt that it was an advantage to find when they've come back into government that there were people like myself whom they knew and trusted, whom they could be certain would work constructively and vigorously with the change of government, irrespective of what my private political views were.

A view from which Denis Healey, for whom Sir Patrick worked a long time ago, does not dissent.

Healey:

You get some people like Sir Humphrey in the television programme *Yes Minister*[1] who basically want to get to the end of their careers without putting a foot wrong, get their knighthood, their CMG and so on, Kindly Call Me God, God Calls Me God [KCMG and GCMG] and all that stuff, but in my experience they are not the majority. I think the people who tend to get to the top have more to them than

---

1 Sir Humphrey Appleby (played by the actor Nigel Hawthorne) was the Permanent Secretary for the Department of Administrative Affairs in the BBC television comedy series *Yes Minister* (*see also* p. 19).

> that. They have this peculiar thing of not wanting to determine policies themselves because if they did they could never survive changes of government.

One can reduce this question about the power of the civil service to two groups of views. One school of thought would disagree with Denis Healey and say that civil servants certainly do want to determine policy; and even if they don't all quite say that, they'd certainly say that the civil service has acquired, and does daily exercise, power, which only a change in the system can overturn and bring back within the bounds of democratic control. There have been stabs at such changes, like the political advisers discussed earlier, but Tony Benn thinks of something much more radical: doing it by the route not of making civil servants more political but making politicians far more like departmental officials, placing not just a couple of ministers in a department but an army of them.

Benn:

> I'm looking again at the old idea that you might actually run departments by ministerial committees of MPs rather than having one or two ministers in the huge machine. I think if you had fifteen Members of Parliament as a ministerial committee and an elected Secretary of State, elected by the parliamentary party as it were, Fred Jowett's[1] old plan, you might make some progress. At the moment it's very, very difficult.

So even the vaulting mind of Mr Benn concedes this might not solve much. We turn to the other school. This says that, irrespective of whether civil servants have views and want to make policy, their power is essentially inertial: they are waiting for a political lead. It's all part of them not wanting to take responsibility any more than they have to. Ministers and only ministers can overcome that inertia, and no fancy new committees or *cabinets* can get round the fact that politics is all about choices, the meat and drink, as Denis Healey says, of a minister's demanding life.

Healey:

> A *cabinet*, a little group of political sympathisers, can't help you against the department, if you haven't got the strength of character or wit to do what you want. They can tell you

1 F. W. Jowett, MP, *What is the Use of Parliament?*, Pass on Pamphlets No. 11, Clarion Press, 1909.

what you ought to do, but you know, having three or four chaps in the central office doesn't help you to deal with the department if you haven't got the strength of character or brain to stand up to them when they're wrong, and I think that ministers can do that if they want to. The great problem, I think, and this is a real problem, is that the nature of government in a democratic country is basically a very difficult choice between competing priorities. You're always short of resources and the government is basically choosing. Now the type of choice you have to make in government is something you cannot learn except in government, and this I think is always going to be the problem about bringing outsiders into government. There may be technical areas, there may be questions of choice which can be hardened and illuminated by outsiders. But the central problem of taking those awful choices, which are usually politically very unpalatable and make you unpopular in your Cabinet and in your government, really depends on the character of the minister. You never get round that.

'Who are the masters now?' we called this last programme in the series. In a sense that's been the question behind all these programmes. What we've heard suggests one answer. It is that the mandarins are the masters, fiercely though they deny it, as long as the argument revolves round how to preserve the status quo, and how to stop the show going off the road. They are the guardians of what they're pleased to call reality, and if reality – immovable facts, unanswerable argument, uncontrollable pressures – is the touchstone, no one is better at coming to its defence than the average civil servant.

Only when so-called reality is under assault, when politicians are not accepting the hallowed definition of it, does real power begin to be transferred from the stoppers to the doers. That's the whole challenge of politics. We want good civil servants but we want good politicians a whole lot more: resilient, cunning and clever enough to outwit the resilient, cunning and clever servants awaiting them. But with one quality more. For the civil service, politics is indeed the art of the possible, but the really successful politician sees that for the inadequate platitude it is. When ministers discover that politics is the art of the impossible, that's the beginning of wisdom: the moment it dawns on them that, as an attitude of mind, 'No, Minister' is not enough.

Postscript

Participating in these programmes was, for Whitehall, a bold thing to do. It exposed civil servants to the public eye in a way they had never been exposed before. It also put them in the hands of a writer and a producer who, in the process of editing interviews, could have done them considerable damage by distorting what they said, either by simplification or over-dramatisation. They ran the risk that popular prejudices, far from being corrected, would be reinforced. To their credit, once the great Whitehall machine, headed by Sir Ian Bancroft, had decided to take that risk, it did so entirely and honourably on the BBC's terms: which stipulated that once an interview was complete it could not be changed or withdrawn, and also that there could be no previews, still less any vetting, of the finished programmes. The politicians, accustomed to giving interviews frequently, would not have given this a second thought. After they had said their piece, most of them probably forgot all about it. For the civil servants it was quite different. Those who spoke – and, one was led to believe, Whitehall generally – took an intense interest in the finished product. And, because it was such a novel venture into their territory, it was their reactions that were the most significant. We decided to carry on the dialogue after the series had been broadcast.

Bancroft was very clear. He said he thought the civil service had been 'hiding its light under a bushel for too long'. Although this rather begged the question of his own encouragement of that habitual reticence, as the most legendary soul of discretion in Whitehall, he had been remarkably candid on the air. Afterwards his view was that the programmes had done well in helping to dispel the 'stereotyped image of the service'. Rather alarmingly, this turned out to be the general verdict of most of the participants. Did this mean the programmes had let the mandarins off too lightly? In the end, to judge from two bits of evidence, probably not. First, we were reassured to learn that Tony Benn, from the opposite end of the spectrum, also thought the exercise had been worthwhile. But secondly, and more interestingly, the general approval of the bureaucrats proved to mask a number of constructive criticisms, which provide a valuable coda to what they said.

Perhaps the most common reservation concerned the depiction the programmes offered of ministers and civil servants as adversaries of each other. Sir Patrick Nairne thought this a serious distortion. *No, Minister*, he said, had taken as its basic concept the idea of a permanent tension between the 'servants in the house' and 'their political masters coming in and out'. 'It was a stimulating, fascinating series of programmes, but I would have thought it right to have taken as your starting point that while of course there would be tensions, fundamentally what you find is a partnership. The real question is not, "Are the civil servants outwitting the politicians, or the politicians outwitting the civil servants?" – like the scenario of the *Barber of Seville* – but rather, "Is this partnership adequately fruitful?" '

Nairne offered examples, from his own experience, of how the civil service, far from preparing itself to baulk a new government, went to great lengths to smooth the path. 'When, as we did not expect, the Conservatives won the election in 1970, we realised at short notice that we were confronted with a government which was going to reverse the policy about defence in south-east Asia. We'd done some homework during the election, even though we thought Labour was going to win. Now the Tories had won, and there was no question of us trying to resist a change in policy. In fact, I remember a ludicrous moment, as some of us sat around a table with the new defence secretary, Lord Carrington, and one of his junior ministers said, "Well, I think we ought to get out of East of Suez." It was me who said with the Secretary of State, "Well, unfortunately that's not the party policy".'

Sir Patrick's other example involved, no doubt, more soul-searching. 'I was personally involved in enormous work at the time of the 1975 referendum on the European Community, on the assumption that Britain might be taken out of it. Even before the Labour government won the election in February 1974, we had been totally prepared, as far as one could be, with detailed papers for dealing with that. We didn't know whether the new government was going to be prepared to work within the treaties. We were crucially concerned to be prepared, even as the election was going on, for the alternatives: renegotiating within, or not within, the treaties.'

All in all, Nairne contended passionately that the whole nature of British government was marked by the responsiveness of the machine to new political masters. Any tension was minor and incidental. Not all his colleagues, however, are quite so dismissive of the 'adversarial' image. One who didn't take part in the programmes, but occupies a senior and sensitive post close to the centre, said he thought such tension a real element in any true picture of government – although not in every ministerial office. 'It exists with particular ministers, particular personalities and, for that matter, with particular officials,' he said. He'd worked for four ministers. 'One of them came in and said he was going to take this place by the scruff of the neck and shake it up. He told us that the way he worked was by butting up against us all the time. With that sort of man, the official is bound to fight back and say here are the facts and here are the arguments, and then very often the minister retreats.'

Three recent ministers who came in very visibly committed to this approach were Tony Benn, at the Departments of Industry and Energy, David Owen at the Foreign Office, and Lord Soames at the Civil Service Department. But internal conflicts can also be more subtle – if no less adversarial. Peter Pooley said: 'You can get Permanent Secretaries not in an adversary role with their minister but with the other civil servants. The head of department needs to defend a minister sometimes from his own inability to see politically important angles. He must tell the civil servants that, despite all their technical objections, this is politically important and the minister's proposal has got to go through.' Minister and Permanent Secretary each had to take the larger view, and see the perspectives beyond their department. 'The two of them can be the only friends each of them has in the world, on occasions, because they equally share that responsibility.'

An aspect of this relationship is, of course, the vexed and elusive one of power. How much power *do* civil servants have? How much will they admit to? On the air, they had been coy about it: almost uniformly so but not, according to Bancroft, by prearrangement. 'There was no collusion between the civil servants taking part,' he said. 'The fact that they did tend to be more consistent in their replies than the politicians is perfectly normal and obvious.' Bancroft remained very strong in his assertion that 'we only have limited power, very limited'. But he did not dissent from Nairne's illuminating and unqualified confession on Programme One that, as Permanent Secretary, his essential power was the power over information. 'There's great importance,' said Bancroft, 'in having the information at the right time and in the right sort of shape, but also making sure your minister shares the information if it is of interest to him. A really very needling question for any civil servant to have flung at him by ministers is, "Why wasn't I told?" '

Sir Donald Maitland put a gloss even on this. He didn't deny that information was power, but doubted whether civil servants had sufficient of a monopoly of it to be all-powerful. 'We are not the sole proprietors of the facts,' he said. Other sources he cited, who bombarded ministers with information (perhaps especially at the Department of Energy?), included pressure groups, commercial lobbies, letter-writers, fellow politicians and the media. Maitland conceded that Nairne's dictum was right in so far as it related to a department's submissions to ministers. But no department could hope to control everything that reached a minister's mind.

Other civil servants, after the event, were less reluctant to admit to their power. 'I think the Hayeses and the Maitlands were mistaken to deny power because they do have power,' said one senior official who did not take part. 'The power of the top official is enormous, if you consider what he is controlling in terms of cash, people, resources, assets. There's positive power and negative power of very considerable importance.' On the other hand, this same official said that it was no match for a politician's power, provided the politician chose to exercise it. 'If you don't have a minister in a department for whatever reason – if he's ill or isn't doing his job, or if there's an election going on or even a Cabinet reshuffle is known to be imminent – you see at once there's a lack of power there. Part of the generator has been switched off.'

Peter Pooley recalled the apparently contradictory conclusions delivered by Tony Benn and Michael Heseltine in Programme One. Benn had lambasted the civil service for its obstructionism, while Heseltine had ridiculed Benn for his inability to master the political forces, in particular the Prime Minister, arrayed against him. 'I think that both Heseltine and Benn were correct,' Pooley said, 'in what they said about the influence the civil service wields, the way it affects the process of government. In that sense there's very real power in the civil service to bring politicians back towards a sensible and practicable and legal and financially responsible line in their policy.' All these were proper objectives, and no civil servant should apologise for them. But Pooley conceded that it did mean that the civil service was pushing politicians towards moderation: 'People aren't going to exercise power with their big stick and start beating ministers about the head. They're beating back the brambles, to stop the minister getting himself cut to bits.'

Nor, said Pooley, were civil servants individually in their jobs because they wanted a sense of power. This raised one of several questions which *No, Minister* had omitted to examine: the question of motivation. Why did people become civil servants? What drove them on to try and be successful ones? Pooley conjured up a picture of a Whitehall in which the wielding of power was not only a discreet and subtle business but something no respectable civil servant would be caught dead actually lusting after. 'One has come across a few colleagues like that, but they're not especially successful in exercising power because they put everyone on their guard. In government, a great many decisions are group decisions, and people like that don't get the co-operation of their colleagues. It's not regarded as very nice to have that sort of ambition – it's not the way we were brought up, it's not professional.' Indeed, a dire fate awaited truly conspicuous power-seekers: 'We're anxious to combat them, crush them, keep them at bay.'

So what *were* they after? 'We're not seeking to increase our power and influence, get ahead over the bodies of other chaps. We're seeking to gain the approval of our colleagues as the chaps who have reached the summit of our profession, and are exercising our professional skills there to the applause of all. That's what one's after.' Although power might exist to some extent, it was a subsidiary factor. 'It's certainly not the money, certainly not the ribbon to stick in your coat. Occasionally power. But professional satisfaction is the main thing. Sometimes my wife thinks it's a hobby we can no longer afford, with a growing family. But she accepts it's what makes me live.'

Nairne – as ever our most liberated contributor among the Permanent Secretaries, but also our acutest critic – felt the whole question of power had been discussed in a two-dimensional way, as if it were simply a matter of distributing power between minister and civil servant. Other factors, he contended, complicated the picture. Three relatively new developments had made a great impression on the daily life of government.

First there was Parliament. His own minister (Patrick Jenkin at that time) had come to power 'rubbing his hands at the thought of what he could do with the government's big majority'. But it was soon apparent that neither the Commons nor the Lords could be regarded as a pushover. This had an important effect on the way policy advice was given by the civil service. 'It means that the defensive role of the civil service is stronger. Civil servants are really very political at the top, in the sense that they don't like sitting round the minister's table and being put down because they are politically naive or inept. One doesn't talk party politics but one does talk House of Commons politics. Civil servants say, more often than they did ten years ago, things like "Yes, but are we going to get that through, Secretary of State?" '

The second contrast was economic, coupled with the influence of the European Community – itself a major limitation on what government departments, whether through ministers or civil servants, could now decide. The change in growth expectations was profound. 'When I was head of the policy and planning division at the Navy department in the Ministry of Defence, we used to discuss whether we could depend on having seven per cent real growth next year in defence spending. It's another world now. It's almost unthinkable that anybody would get anything like that these days. Even in a social department like DHSS you're struggling to get between one and two per cent.'

A third factor, however, possibly pointed more directly to a transfer of power away from politicians. This was technology: getting more complex every year and hence further and further out of reach of the average minister. 'In the Defence area, a minister has got to be able to stand up to the admirals and the scientists. Even if he does his homework he'll find that very difficult. On civil nuclear power it takes an awful lot to stand up to the head of Harwell and to those Department of Energy civil servants who've been in it for years. To have a real grasp of social security legislation requires an enormous amount of technical expertise: to tell civil servants that they've got it wrong, or the party's plans aren't as difficult as they say.' On this front Sir Patrick was disposed to concede that the politician – the very function of the politician as against that of the bureaucrat – was under threat: 'I do honestly think that the terms of trade, so to speak, have moved in favour of the official.'

But is even the typical official best trained and equipped to handle expert knowledge? On this score surely the line between political and official competence could not be drawn that sharply? In Programme Three we had asked whether civil servants were incompetent. On the whole they were very little criticised, at least by their various political masters. Discussing this question afterwards with officials who had not taken part, we struck a vein of self-criticism matching that exposed by, for example, Sir Derek Rayner. In particular, the supremacy of the 'generalist' came under strong attack in one discussion of what makes good civil servants. 'The young civil servant is given the impression, as soon as he has joined, that what matters are his wits rather than his knowledge. He will never have to take another examination as long as he's in the service, or even pass any quantifiable test in the way a young businessman does. This tends to make the young civil servant think training is a bit of a joke, maybe giving him some useful knowledge but not requiring him to be graded or anything like that. He's going to be moved from job to job, and not encouraged to master particular fields or subjects, or develop a pattern of relationships with people outside the department.' This tradition of the all-rounder, said this official, bred cynicism and 'a lack of commitment to subject matter'. Two things should be done. 'First, we have to tell them that they're going to have to acquire certain knowledge, and demonstrate it by examination early on. Secondly, we must make them get their hands very dirty.'

Admittedly, the speaker himself showed no sign of having had much grime beneath his finger-nails. But he was clear what kind of dirty work the high-fliers of the future should be made to do. 'They should go and manage district offices of the DHSS. They should work in social service departments and in industry. Remember, a lot of these people have moved from a protected atmosphere at home and school to a similar atmosphere at university, into what is a very private and comfortable atmosphere inside the service.'

To the point about expertise, however, Patrick Nairne had a ready answer. He clearly believes that as problems get more complex ministers may find themselves even further out of their depth. But there are strict limits, in his view, to what the real experts can be expected to do. Here, in its modern incarnation, is the old theory of the supreme generalist:

'I am one of those Permanent Secretaries who's worked at the top of two big departments – Defence and DHSS – filled with good professionals. What it's taught me is that the outstanding professionals cannot get right to the top of their own profession, because at that level they are no longer the best. They want to be the Chief Medical Officer or the Chief Scientific Adviser or the Chief Engineer or whatever it may be. If they were going to have the least chance of becoming even a Deputy Secretary they've got to come out of their profession at an earlier stage and get some experience of working in the rather different type of administrative/political environment, which they've been on the whole protected from when they were working as professionals. They've probably got to do a job as a Private Secretary. They may have to get experience working in one of the central departments. Certainly they've got to have the laborious and rather exacting experience of being the head of a branch, subjected to the daily battering of parliamentary questions, the sudden requirement to produce a speech for the adjournment debate, putting through a Bill and all that. To think, in other words, that an outstanding engineer or doctor or scientist can suddenly come over and be an effective Deputy Secretary, often perhaps giving advice to the minister alone and under great pressure, without having had any of that experience lower down, is, I think, totally naive. The result is that when you look around Whitehall today, you don't find any people in that position, except in the very, very rare case.'

We had also explored whether these high-fliers, from wherever they came, were accountable for what they did. As Programme Four tried to make clear, this question reaches to the heart of the constitution. Listeners were provided with some rich linguistic agonising. Nairne, for example, drew the distinction between being 'accountable' and being 'answerable', with the object of asserting that while civil servants could not supersede ministers as the people ultimately responsible to Parliament ('accountable'), they should not be regarded as having to answer to nobody: they were therefore 'answerable'. Sir Patrick repeated this distinction when we saw him later: 'I feel I've rather created it myself,' he said. With the benefit of time to consult the *Oxford English Dictionary*, we made the perhaps unsurprising discovery that the primary meaning it assigns to each of these words is in fact identical. 'Accountable' and 'answerable' both mean: 'Liable to be called to account: responsible.' Nonetheless, one can see what Sir Patrick was groping for.

Two younger but senior officials who did not take part in *No, Minister* cut through the ambiguities of Programme Four with some severity. In different ways they both observed that officials were insufficiently accountable for what they did, and believed British administration would be improved if this timeless tradition were re-examined. 'I can think of clear examples of unhelpful advice being given,' said one. 'Not deliberately, but simply because the official wasn't equipped, didn't have the necessary experience or whatever. And there's no sanction. Nothing in practice does happen. People may get shunted off sideways. But there's certainly no financial sanction. Particularly in the top reaches, the sort of differentials in pay don't make any odds anyway. I think that's very sad. It's very easy to say we have to produce the answers to all these parliamentary questions, and appear before select committees. But that's got nothing to do with accountability at all. There ought to be ways of motivating people, to make it sensible for them to be accountable, to *want* to be accountable.'

This official had no clear ideas about how to create such a punitive regime. He simply felt the lack of it. The second official was more emphatic. He said that true accountability depended on co-operation between politicians and their departments. First, the politicians. 'They must tell us what they want. We need to say quite clearly to ministers, "Look, minister, don't let's go on pussy-footing about. Let's be clear what our management function is, as we see it. Do you agree that we've got it right?" '

On that basis civil servants, especially at the very top, should be able to point to their successes and failures. This should be a public process. 'I think the minister and the department would be greatly helped if, at the end of each year, the Permanent Secretary came to the minister and said, "This is what I've done this year, this is my account of my stewardship. I've saved this, I've reformed that. I've succeeded here and I've failed there. And I'm very happy for you to publish this account." Now don't get me wrong. I don't believe there's a great panting audience out there waiting for all this. But Parliament and the press would have their confidence greatly increased. The good things should be brought out as well as the bad. People deserve to be publicly identified and have their work praised and noted.'

Nor was it essential for the discrimination between good and bad to be entirely theoretical. 'We're talking not only about a clear commission for the Permanent Secretary but about a system of rewards and penalties for individual civil servants. If the signals you're getting in your pay-packet are that it doesn't really matter whether you're good, bad or indifferent, we're not going to get an effective and lasting change.'

This kind of evaluation could even be applied to the sacred and imponderable area of policy advice, not just 'management'. Here, admittedly, there was no getting away from the unquantifiable matter of 'judgement'. But a change in the pattern of civil service work would lead to better results. It all linked up with the need to abandon such swift movement of generalists from post to post. 'If a man is doing a policy function for two-and-a-half years and he's going to be off and over the hill by the time the policy takes effect, that's one thing. But if you say to Mr X, "Advise me on this policy", and Mr X is going to be responsible for implementing it and seeing it through for five or six years, that's going to have some influence on his judgement, and I would think for the better.'

Important an innovation though this would be, it is not addressed to the ultimate test the civil service might soon have to face. We did not confront this directly in *No, Minister* either, although it was implicit in several of the programmes. It is the question of how Whitehall would respond to a truly radical government, determined to overthrow all the props of 'centrist' orthodoxy as they have been erected in post-war Britain: a Labour government, in other words, pursuing what have come to be known as Bennite policies on the economy, Europe and defence. Tony Benn himself said in the last programme that it would be essential to politicise the civil service by creating committees of Labour MPs to supervise the work of each department. But to what extent would this transform the service as we know it? Sir Ian Bancroft did not doubt that the service would respond as it always has (he claimed) to a new political imperative. As long as the mandarins were left in place, he said, they would do the job. 'I think the danger would come if one found very large numbers of political advisers appointed who were not only advisers to ministers but were also put in line of command over large numbers of civil servants.' Committees of MPs would be equally bad. 'The greater the number of politicians concentrated in one department, not the greater the strength but the greater the discord. It's a very rum idea. As I understand Mr Benn, he was talking in terms of equality of powers, not with one chap as ringmaster cracking the whip.

I don't think that's any good, any more than I would think it a good idea, instead of having a Permanent Secretary, to have a committee of Permanent Secretaries.'

One very senior mandarin who had listened in was even more profoundly scornful. He thought that if administration was to be politicised in this way it would not only be inefficient but would actually kill off the senior civil service as we know it. The Bennite system, he thought, would soon mean that Whitehall ceased to be a place where high-fliers saw themselves having a worthwhile career. They would either become frightened of being turfed out if they crossed the Labour party, or would know there was a ceiling above which they could not hope to rise as professional non-party public officials.

On the air, not one civil servant was other than confident that the service would try and serve a radical Labour government as faithfully as it had served any other. Sir Michael Butler, the UK ambassador to the European Communities, hinted at a different point: that he personally might resign rather than work for an anti-European government. Nevertheless it is true that the professionalism of the service might see almost all its members through – although not without the help of a lot of dexterous manoeuvring in the name of reality, continuity and the like. Some officials, however, see such an eventuality as presenting a deeper problem. One of them is Peter Pooley.

'I don't think the civil service could cope. They'd be dealing with matters way beyond their range of reference, and ministers would have to buttress themselves not just with *cabinets* but with a much larger unit for advice and implementation. I mean people who could brush civil servants on one side and keep them out of the room, only to emerge now and then to say, "This is what has been decided and bloody well get on with it". The civil service is not well made to cope with ruthless, reforming zeal.'

A point perhaps well epitomised by Sir Patrick Nairne. Sir Patrick approved of the programmes – on the whole. He was extraordinarily helpful in persuading his colleagues to take part. The only thing that really disappointed him was the conclusion. So, as a final gift to us, he wrote his own conclusion, to set beside the original (see page 98). It reveals that mastery of drafting which is still perhaps the mandarin's distinctive hallmark. By changing only a small number of words, he has altered the sense in very much the way an incoming minister might require a draft prepared for his predecessor to be altered. In tribute to Sir Patrick, let him have the last word:

' "Who are the masters now?" we call the last programme in our series. In a sense that's been the question behind all these programmes. What we've heard suggests, I think, one answer: it is that the mandarins are the masters so long as the factors of reality and continuity are allowed to condition, or have to condition, what ministers are seeking to do. If reality – immovable facts, unanswerable argument, uncontrollable pressures – is to be the touchstone, or continuity of policies – the need to reap what a previous administration has sown or not to change what the public has come to accept or expect – is to be regarded as paramount, then no one is better at fostering and defending the policies to be followed than the average civil servant. Only when ministers are determined to pursue new, and perhaps radical, policies – challenging the arguments of reality and continuity in the process – will the politicians exercise real power and be effectively on top. The promotion of policy change is the principal challenge of politics. We want good civil servants to identify the factors of reality, and to make clear any disadvantages of discontinuity; but, even more, we want good politicians who will be determined, clever, and if necessary cunning enough to harness the intellect, energy and imagination of civil servants to the task of overcoming the obstacles which too cautious a view of reality, or too great an emphasis on continuity, can sometimes place in the path of the government. For both minister and civil servants politics remains the art of the possible. But the beginning of wisdom for the politicians is the discovery that the greatest success in politics depends on transforming into the possible what seems to be impossible. For that an attitude of mind confined to "No, Minister" on the part of their civil servants can never be enough.'

Index